RICK ELSTEIN'S
TENNIS KINETICS

with
MARTINA NAVRATILOVA

by Rick Elstein
and Mary Carillo Bowden

WITH AN INTRODUCTION BY
Martina Navratilova

SIMON AND SCHUSTER
New York

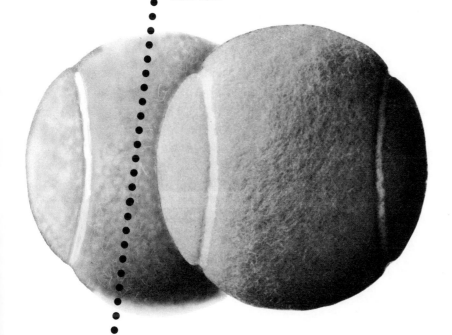

A WORD ABOUT THE EXERCISES IN THIS BOOK—The Tennis Kinetics drills and fitness exercises are designed to build rhythm and quickness. Some of them are strenuous. Before beginning either the drill or exercise program, consult with your personal physician.

Copyright © 1985 by Rick Elstein's Tennis Kinetics, Inc.
All rights reserved
including the right of reproduction
in whole or in part in any form
Published by Simon and Schuster
A Division of Simon & Schuster, Inc.
Simon & Schuster Building
Rockefeller Center
1230 Avenue of the Americas
New York, New York 10020
SIMON AND SCHUSTER and colophon are registered trademarks of
Simon & Schuster, Inc.
RICK ELSTEIN'S TENNIS KINETICS is a registered trademark of Rick Elstein's Tennis
Kinetics, Inc.
Designed by Stanley S. Drate/Folio Graphics Co., Inc.
Manufactured in the United States of America
10 9 8 7 6 5 4 3 2 1
Library of Congress Cataloging in Publication Data
Elstein, Rick.
   Rick Elstein's Tennis Kinetics with Martina
Navratilova.

   1. Tennis.   II. Tennis—Training.   I. Navratilova,
Martina, DATE –.   II. Bowden, Mary Carillo.
III. Title.   IV. Title: Tennis Kinetics with Martina
Navratilova.
GV995.E43   1985   796.342'2   85-8331
ISBN: 0-671-55540-5

ACKNOWLEDGMENTS

Martina Navratilova has proven many times that her championship style is not reserved for the court alone. She is the ultimate professional in every way. We express our deepest gratitude to her for her time, effort, and friendship. She is a very special person.

Fred McEwan has contributed greatly to the Tennis Kinetics program during the last few years. His hard work on this book is greatly appreciated.

Sections and chapters concerned with physical fitness and with questions of sports medicine and body mechanics are based very much on the contributions of three notable experts in the field of physical therapy and sports medicine.

David O. Balsley, R.P.T., M.Ed., is Director, Sports Medicine Performance and Research Center, at the Hospital of Special Surgery–Cornell Medical Center. His work with college and professional athletes—including players for the New York Mets, Giants, and Islanders and the St. John's basketball team—has been credited as instrumental in the prevention of injuries.

Donald Alan Chu, R.P.T., Ph.D., has been Professor of Kinesiology and Physical Education at California State University (Hayward) since 1969. He is one of the pioneers of plyometrics, a type of training which develops strength and speed, and which is embodied in many of the exercises in this book.

Robert A. Panariello, M.S., R.P.T., A.T.C., is an NATA Certified Athletic Trainer, Sports Medicine Performance and Research Center, at the Hospital of Special Surgery–Cornell Medical Center. He has established, with Donald Chu and strength coach Johnny Parker, plyometric training programs for the St. Johns University basketball team and the New York Giants football team respectively.

The cover photograph of Rick Elstein was done by Adam J. Stoltman.

The photography throughout this book, including the cover photograph of Martina Navratilova, is the work of Russ Adams, whose professional manner is greatly appreciated.

The line drawings were done by Jackie Aher. We couldn't have asked for a better job.

Special thanks to Sue Hawkins and Morton and Cherie Jonap for all their help.

Finally, our deep appreciation to Don Hutter, senior editor at Simon & Schuster. His professional guidance and expertise brought everything together.

To my wife, Margot, daughter, Julie, and my dear friends Herman Gross and Irving Glick. Their love, support, and wisdom made Tennis Kinetics possible.

—RICK ELSTEIN

To my wonderful husband, Bill.

—MARY CARILLO BOWDEN

CONTENTS

INTRODUCTION

by Martina Navratilova

There are two questions I seem to get asked all the time—"What are your goals?" and "How much better can you get?" My answer to both questions is the same—I want to keep improving every part of my game. And in the last few years I have really learned *how* to improve. I am fit and disciplined and more technically aware of my game than ever before, and with hard work and good coaching it is my hope to get better and better for as long as I play this game.

For many years I played tennis using only my natural abilities and instincts, so when I finally took to overhauling my game there was virtually no aspect of it that did not undergo change or reevaluation. I relearned grips, spins, serves, and tactics. The days of arriving on court and waiting for divine inspiration were over. After fifteen years of playing tennis I was just starting to learn things for the first time, and the new knowledge was challenging and exciting.

One of my biggest revelations occurred in 1982 when I met Rick Elstein. A two-hour practice session had been arranged with Rick, and after hitting with him on the first day I was moving better than I ever had. You must understand that even when I'd been out of shape I'd been quick around the court, and at the time I was already one of the fastest players on the women's circuit. But as with so many other players my court movement was intuitive, instinctive; and since I had never really thought much about my style of movement there were parts that were quick but incorrect, automatic but inefficient. Rick introduced me to Tennis Kinetics and made me keenly aware of the importance of proper body movement for maximum results.

Relearning the movements the right way was easy because Tennis Kinetics reduces the game of tennis to its basic elements and rhythms, and when you put them together you get the chain of motion necessary for control and power—you get *kinetic*. A "kinetic chain" is the way in which a body moves in order to produce an athletic event. In tennis the stroke begins from the feet

INTRODUCTION BY MARTINA NAVRATILOVA. . . . .

12

and legs, transfers to the hips and torso, and finally affects the shoulders and arms. It is this progression of forces that creates the powerful and accurate movement required for tennis. Without this correct chain a player is reduced to hitting with uncoordinated motions, less power, and diminished accuracy, and can injure himself as well.

As you must already realize, each stroke you make takes time to execute. Tennis Kinetics teaches you how to create the time you need in order to hit your best shots. You will learn that every movement has its own importance and value, and that you gain or lose opportunities, balance, court positions, and options with every move you make. The proper kinetic chain gives you that most valued element of tennis—*time*.

The first section of this book introduces you to the world of Tennis Kinetics and explains the basic elements and rhythms of the sport. The second section provides the reader with his own personal developmental program, a program remarkable for its scope and clarity. There are dozens of drills for all different levels of play, followed by a fitness section that offers everything a tennis player needs to get in shape and stay that way. Finally, there is a section on tactics and strategy, with the last chapter we call "The Look"—a series of photos of myself using the Tennis Kinetics method in top tournament play: at Wimbledon in 1984.

Tennis Kinetics is full of original thoughts on the game. It is truly a whole new way of looking at tennis. And while the principles of Tennis Kinetics are scientific, learning it is easy and fun, whether you're a beginner or a pro like me. As I've said, my goal is to keep improving. If your goal is the same, do what I did. *Get kinetic.* This book will show you how.

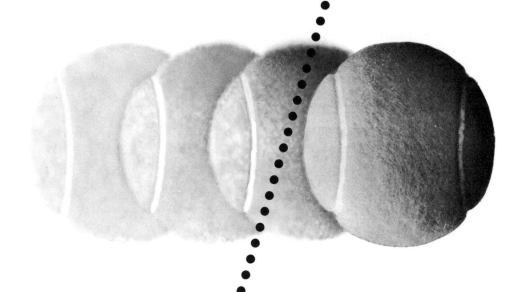

ONE

BASIC TENNIS KINETICS

1 | WHAT IS TENNIS KINETICS?

kinetics, ki·net'iks, *n* Relating to motion: imparting or growing out of motion.
—*Webster's Dictionary*

All sports are kinetic, whether they are high-speed sports such as ice hockey and basketball, or low-speed sports such as bowling. All relate to motion, and require skills that employ motion. Many sports combine several different skills. A hockey player must skate and, at the same time, be able to shoot the puck; a basketball player must be able to dribble the ball past his opponents before he shoots for the hoop; a bowler must coordinate stance, rhythm, and balance to produce a smooth and accurate ball release. The quality of kinetic production—of energetic, controlled motion—is the very essence of sports such as figure skating and gymnastics, in which the judge's cards declare the winner. In other sports where winning performance is more obviously determined—as in track-and-field competition, in which the winner will break the tape or jump the highest or throw the javelin the farthest—superior kinetics is also crucial.

In every sport the skills involved are developed in proportion to their importance, both separately and in combination. An ice hockey player will practice shooting the puck, taking a check, and giving a pass, all the while honing his skating skills. Without powerful skating a hockey player cannot be in control of the puck.

Tennis Kinetics takes a new approach to the development of tennis skills by exploiting its constituents as a kinetic sport, a sport of motion. Hitting the ball is a kinetic event, but so are reaction to the ball, movement to the ball, and recovery after the ball is struck.

BASIC TENNIS KINETICS. . . . .

16

Traditionally, tennis has been considered almost solely a hitting sport, and emphasis has long been placed on hitting in the teaching of the game. Yet only 10 percent of one's time on the tennis court involves the hitting of the ball, even while players seem to spend 100 percent of their court time developing their hitting skills.

We would like to change your perception of tennis, to show you how to develop great hitting skills the right way— through proper movement. The common denominator among the best tennis players in the world is their great movement on the court, but because of the nature of the game, a tennis player's speed and footwork tend to be overlooked by most spectators. Whereas basketball, hockey, and boxing involve the competitors in a close-quartered duel of speed and agility, tennis players are often eighty feet apart. Thus, a spectator will track the ball from one side of the net to the other and often fail to see the movement before and after the racket makes contact with the ball. Yet if an observer were to trace the errors of a typical match, he would find that the majority are caused by kinetic mistakes before the actual stroke.

The best players in the world move as well as they hit. With most lesser players the difference between their hitting game and their running game is fantastically one-sided. Players who move well control the ball, while players who are rushed and out of position will continually be in trouble. Tennis Kinetics can dramatically change the level of your total game, quickly and for good. It's fun, easy to understand, and, best of all, it works.

Perhaps you've noticed how, after you watch the pros play tennis, your own games tends to improve. While you watch you are unconsciously assimilating their movements, stroking patterns, and built-in rhythms. Tennis Kinetics is based on the building of *muscle memory*. In the course of repeating correct movements and rhythms, the quality of a player's movement draws equal to his hitting. We have found that through Tennis Kinetics the average player's rate of improvement is remarkable, and that as the player's movement skills improve his hitting game improves as well.

Tennis Kinetics was not originally intended to be put into use by the likes of Martina Navratilova. The study of kinetics in tennis began with an eye toward injury rehabilitation and prevention. The key participants in this study were Rick Elstein, Dr. Irving Glick, physical therapist David Balsley, and the late Dr. John Marshall. In 1979 Dr. Glick, Dr. Marshall, and David Balsley began to review the cases of injured athletes to determine the cause of injuries and the means of rehabilitation so that the injury would not recur. Their studies focused mainly on weight-bearing joints, such as the knee and ankle, and also dealt with lower back injuries. They found that an athlete's movement was very much responsible, if not for the original injury, then for the chance of reinjury. Correct movement was in fact essential to postoperative patients whose every step was an adventure in terror.

Through seventeen years of teaching and coaching dozens of world-class players, Rick Elstein had always felt that movement is key to the game of tennis. When the Tennis Kinetics study began, he was working with a couple of athletes who required knee surgery. He joined forces with the study group to get these players back on the court fit, stronger, and as far more efficient players. The most pleasant side effect of this rehabilitation effort, Elstein discovered, was that healthy movement made for better performance, and on that premise he was able to develop a program of Tennis Kinetics training that transcended the limited world of injured tennis players. The program grew popular, and many top players learned the Tennis Kinetics method and raised their games. Billie Jean King sharpened her reaction time and technical awareness; Bonnie Gadusek, Melissa Brown, Jo Anne Russell, and the O'Reilly triplets improved quickly and easily. Martina reached a class by herself. Now it's your turn.

2 THE IMPORTANCE OF KINETICS IN TENNIS

To better appreciate the importance of proper movement, we would like to offer an overview of the *kinetic chain,* the sequence that produces power and control in sports. As a tennis player, you know that impact of the ball imposes substantial forces on your racket. To control these forces the body must counteract with forces of its own. Most tennis players attack the ball with wrist and forearm, but the strength generated by these small muscle groups is not nearly enough to produce a powerful and controlled reply. In fact, the movements necessary to master the racket and ball are similar to those required in boxing, in throwing a shot or discus, in pitching a baseball, or passing a football. The basic principles of projecting an object through space are found in a number of athletic events, and by exploring the dynamics of movement we can learn a lot about the sport of tennis.

The discus throw and shot put involve the thrusting of an object for distance. These events require much of an athlete, as he must generate maximum force in order to produce maximum distance and performance. His body is the sole source of power, his movements the only means of generating force. The sequence of movements he makes is called a "kinetic chain."

We know that the discus thrower does not just stand there, arbitrarily flexing certain muscles and waiting for something glorious to happen. The kinetic chain he must employ is a process, a sequence of rotational movements that begins in the lower limbs

Professional boxer Greg Walsh prepares to throw a punch. Power is generated by rotating the hips and shoulders . . . followed by full extension of the hand.

College pitcher Steve Woods is ready to generate power, beginning in the legs . . . rotating his hips and trunk . . . followed by his shoulders, arm, and wrist, completing the kinetic chain.

and ends in the upper limbs. The rotation of these moving parts generates and increases the velocity of each succeeding muscle group. The forces are transferred from the back foot to the hips, trunk, shoulders, arm, and finally the wrist, resulting in the discus's propulsion from the body.

Any athlete who can develop such tremendous power from such a kinetic chain can also develop pinpoint control. A baseball pitcher, a boxer, and a football quarterback need both. Sports such as these require power for speed and distance and enough control to be accurate to within several inches at long distances.

As the body parts increase in velocity and rotational forces build throughout the system, a harmonious blend of power and control is achieved by the athlete. Every tennis player strives for the one-two combination of power and control, but in an effort to hit harder, most players sacrifice their control of the ball. Through the illustrations in this chapter, we can see what happens at the point of contact, and therein identify the problems of this sport and their solutions.

Tennis, like baseball, involves the use of an instrument with which to hit the ball. Since the body does not have direct contact with and control of the oncoming object, the athlete must generate power and control through this intermediary tool of the sport. So in tennis as in baseball the athlete's first concern is to master his hitting tool. Both the ball and the body deliver forces to the instrument, and for the briefest of instants—the moment of impact—both ball and body fight for control. All too often, in both baseball and tennis, the ball wins the fight.

Let's examine what effect the impact of the tennis ball can have upon the racket.

Research indicates that the forces of impact exerted by a tennis ball at normal speed are substantial enough so that any kind of off-center contact cannot be equalized by the forces generated in the hand, wrist, and forearm. You can hold the racket in a virtual death grip, but the outcome will be the same—you will lose control of the ball and create errors, whether they be sitters just over the net, half-gainers into the net, or bazookas over the baseline.

It is obvious that the body must increase its influence at the moment of impact. So what's the answer? Most players increase the length and speed of their swing. Bad idea. Even at higher speeds the arm, wrist, and hand are incapable of controlling the racket's response to the ball; they will still respond negatively to

Off-center contact. The result is
an opening of the racket face
and loss of control.

When the ball controls the
racket face, causing it to open
or close, the effect is known as
"torque."

the forces of impact. Too large a backswing requires split-second precision in producing an accurate kinetic chain. Because it takes so much time, it greatly inhibits a player's ability to perform basic shots such as return of serve, approach shots, volleys, or even deep groundstrokes. Repeated attempts to increase force in this way create undo stress and are major causes of injury, particularly tennis elbow. The solution is what could be called a holistic approach to hitting through the kinetic chain.

Let's examine the kinetic chain for stroking a tennis ball in detail. To produce the process correctly takes about a half second, so the sequence is very important.

As photo series below indicates, the sequence of movements begins with the lower extremity (everything below the hips) and transfers through the hips, trunk (spine, abdomen), shoulder, forearm, wrist, and hand. The movement is a rotational one, much like a spiral. Rotation is the body's method of increasing velocity and momentum of the joint closest to the racket while maintaining smooth relationships among all the joints and body parts. You have seen similar forces at work in a popular ice skating game—the whip. In the whip, a long line of skaters forms in the middle of a pond, skating ever more quickly in a circle. The skater farthest

The kinetic chain for the forehand groundstroke. Notice the difference in the hip and shoulder positions from the first photo to Contact in the second.

1

2

from the center develops the greatest speed (and gets the best ride) because he is being whipped into increasing velocities and gets the biggest kinetic backlash of the group. So it is in the kinetic chain of tennis. Through rotation of the hips and trunk, one continues the velocity started in the lower extremity and terminated through the shoulders, arm, and hand. Thus, the total force is transmitted through the hand to the racket itself—the end of the whip.

Let's take a look at how tennis compares with other sports in terms of "kinetic events." A discus or shot put event may require six to twelve throws in a meet. Starting pitchers throw from ninety to one hundred baseballs on a good day; and batters step up to the plate four or five times during a game and swing four, maybe five times each at bat, on a good day getting two hits. Quarterbacks on good teams throw twenty completions out of thirty passes. In two sets of tennis a player will average three hundred to four hundred contacts with the ball, and that number quadruples in advanced play and on slower courts. When you look at tennis this way, you realize that a few errors here and there shouldn't be upsetting, but more to the point, there is greater opportunity on a tennis court for factors that interfere with or impede the quality of a kinetic chain.

3

4

BASIC TENNIS KINETICS. . . . .

26

Of these factors, the biggest one is the constraint of time. In the other sports we've mentioned the athlete has time to ready himself physically and mentally for the event. A batter can take some practice swings, loosen up a bit, even step out of the box if he feels the need for more time. Likewise, a pitcher, quarterback, discus thrower, or shot-putter can pace himself for the moment of truth. Tennis players normally have about four seconds or less between shots in a rally, and must continue to produce shots until the point is ended. But it does not stop there. A tennis player does not know where he will be making his plays from shot to shot. Most of his returns will probably be within twenty feet of his last shot, but again, he will only have about two seconds or less to get to the next ball. It gets a little complicated out there sometimes. A baseball player would have a lot more on his mind if his sport were more like tennis. Imagine a batter swinging every four seconds, six times in a row, from a floating home plate. (Now *there's* a national pastime.)

Up to now we have put the thrust of the kinetic chain on the actual point of contact, but while vital to tennis, the act of making contact with the ball represents only 10 percent of the activity on the court. The fact that a tennis player has so little time and so much distance to cover makes him less like a baseball batter than an infielder, a player who must be prepared to field a hit every three or four seconds and make a good throw to first base. He may have a terrific kinetic chain for throwing, but if he fails to get to the ball in time and to position himself to use that chain, he will make errors. If he can move with expertise and efficiency to every ball, he will find that he need not always summon up his best throw to be a good player. In fact, his expert movement around the field will only complement his throwing style.

In tennis one's ability to produce good kinetic chains is directly dependent upon the ability to maneuver around the court. Every action on the court has an effect on the quality of one's game. When moving well, you are not only hitting a better shot, you are also eliciting from your opponent a lesser shot from a weaker court position. This double effect underscores the importance of Tennis Kinetics, inasmuch as it can make the difference between running down an opponent's angle or cutting the shot off for a putaway. Remember that what you do before you hit the ball is either helping you or helping your opponent; there is always some effect. If you are late to recover to the proper court position after your shot, you give your opponent more room in which to play his next shot. It then becomes increasingly harder for you to properly defend your court, while on the other side of the net your opponent has many choices and much less pressure. This can severely affect the cleverness and imagination of your spins, speeds, and angles, for it is hard to be nimble of mind and body when you're up against the wall. Where you hit from and where you hit to are jointly the result of your running abilities. That's why Tennis Kinetics will give you greater control of your opponent's game as well as your own. Moreover, Tennis Kinetics is the most efficient way to use energy and offers the least amount of stress on the body, as Dr. Glick and David Balsley explain in the following sections.

THE IMPORTANCE OF KINETICS FOR FITNESS
....

Doctor Irving Glick is a sports medicine authority, an orthopedist, and physician to many of the world's top tennis players. He helped to develop Tennis Kinetics and says of the system:

> The Tennis Kinetics program is the ideal way to prepare one's body for playing tennis. It develops speed, agility, quickness, and balance, and it improves flexibility and strength while building cardiovascular fitness. These are the physical characteristics a tennis player must develop to perform well.

A steady regimen of running is a fine cardiovascular workout and promotes general fitness, but it does not address the needs of a tennis player. (It's hard to believe that a marathon runner could poop out on the tennis court, but it's happened.) First of all, the rhythm of distance running is opposite to the rhythm of tennis movement, which involves starts and stops, changing tempos and directions, and a constant variety of cadence and size of steps. The jogger runs in a heel-toe fashion, whereas a tennis player is constantly on the balls of his feet. Furthermore, regular running does not involve the all-important aspect of recovery, a built-in feature of a tennis match. While sprint work can help a tennis player, it still fails to approximate the directional changes of tennis. The agility drills in Tennis Kinetics not only replicate the speed and motion of the sport, they also train the body's recovery system. You should keep in mind that regular running trains your body with an energy system that you rarely use in tennis. Distance running involves the aerobic system, which uses oxygen as its fuel source. On the tennis court it takes several minutes of play before the aerobic system kicks in, and until it does, the body draws its

BASIC TENNIS KINETICS . . . .

28

energy from its anaerobic system. The fuel source of anaerobics is energy that is already stored in the body, and since rallies rarely last more than a minute, it is with this system that the tennis player performs. The emphasis of his training should be on quickness and fast recovery, on the capacity of his anaerobic metabolism to replenish itself after short bursts of speed. That's why the Tennis Kinetics program can make your current running program obsolete.

THE IMPORTANCE OF KINETICS IN THE PREVENTION OF INJURY

When Rick Elstein began working with physical therapist David Balsley, a new dimension was added to his teaching methods. Medical knowledge of a player's mobility is the key to injury prevention and rehabilitation, and since injuries occur for many reasons, Tennis Kinetics was developed to apply to a player's entire motion, not merely his more troublesome strokes.

If you have ever been injured on or off the court, you already know that even a localized pain can affect the entire body and, as a medical analogy, infect the healthiest areas of your game. The tennis elbow that you developed while experimenting with your topspin backhand could subvert your killer serve. Getting to a ball late, or being caught out of position (for whatever reason you failed to execute the proper kinetic chain), can mean hurting yourself by using small, quick muscles instead of the major muscle groups; the result can be pulled tendons, stretched ligaments, or worse. David Balsley speaks about the most common injuries in tennis and why they occur:

> Mostly we get muscle-tendon, ligamentous, and patella problems. Before he died, Dr. John Marshall was starting to study ligament laxity in female tennis players. He thought that there was a correlation between loose-jointed tennis players and anterior crusciate ligaments [which help stabilize the knee] that give out. A person who is loose-jointed is susceptible to injury when caught in the wrong position with a leg out straight and a heel down on the ground. If this player was in a stationary position and happened to have her knee locked instead of flexed, she would not only be slower were she to move, she would also be in danger of popping a ligament. You must always be aware of what your body is doing, always be on your toes.
>
> Tennis Kinetics keeps you from being rushed. The danger of getting rushed is that you are not physically or mentally ready to take off. Physically, a rushed shot usually originates in the knees, rather than in the hips. You might rotate your knees instead of your hips in reaction to a shot, and if the ligament does not respond well

. . . .**THE IMPORTANCE OF KINETICS IN TENNIS**

29

to the stress, you can force the patella to shift in a way that irritates the kneecap. You have less chance of predicting how long it will take you to get to a ball when rushed, so the tendency is to force yourself to take off quicker. In an effort to make up for lost time, you explode off your mark, which tends to pull muscles. If you have to run this fast, you must remember that taking off quickly means slowing down quickly. Your momentum is carrying you too fast, too far forward because your body doesn't have time to accommodate the jerky motion. This can cause irritation to the cartilage or dislodging the cartilage in the knee, sprained ankles, or any number of injuries. Lack of stabilization occurs in the upper body as well, and often explains tennis elbow problems. *When you are late to the ball, you rob yourself of the chance to use the muscle mass and stability of your shoulder, and your elbow alone takes the force of the ball as you swing.* Wrist problems can occur for the same reason. Lower back problems come when you try to sprint from a straight-up position. This puts a high-velocity muscle contraction on the back without warning your neuromuscular system of the complicated move. This causes pulled muscles and other irritations.

Tennis Kinetics trains players in total movement, physically and mentally. From a physiological standpoint, *if you are late mentally you will be late physically*. If the brain is not ready to fire, the muscles will not be ready either. All impulses come from the brain, and you cannot move a muscle unless the brain tells that muscle to move. Tennis Kinetics trains the body and the mind to be on target and ready to go. The brain must be uncluttered—have very narrow vision—so that it can focus in on the ball and clue the body early to the proper moves. This can be learned by anyone at any level of the game. Sometimes it involves deprogramming your old speed of mind and foot, but this is not a difficult process. From a neurological standpoint, if you train a joint to move at a certain speed, that joint's nerve endings will send impulses to the brain, and the brain learns that speed of motion. The muscles will contract as quickly or as slowly as you train them to act. If you wish to play serve-and-volley tennis, your brain and body must learn the required speed and must train at that speed.

David Balsley works with all kinds of athletes and enjoys comparing and contrasting different motions found in different sports. He explains how some of these athletes train by way of pointing out the training needs of tennis players:

Wrestlers warm up slowly and deliberately. First they practice all the simple moves—warm up their arms and legs and focus their center of gravity. Then they use other people to try to knock them off center, off balance—to upset their equilibrium so that they can't complete the movement. They go from practicing alone to a "loading" situation [with someone else], then a situation with different moves, then a sequence of moves. If you skip moves or

BASIC TENNIS KINETICS. . . . .

30

perform some of them incorrectly, you will lose because your opponent will pick up the weak link and nail you for it.

In dance, body control is the key element. It sounds odd, but to control movement we use a lot of inhibiting factors. If a dancer were to let everything go, there would be no symmetry, no control. A dancer must practice eccentric loads, which means he must contract the muscles as he is lengthening them. This is very difficult to do but very necessary, and common in sports as well. Most parts of the body are regulated by inhibitors. In baseball, one of the regulators of how fast your arm moves is how well you can slow it down, which is one function of the rotator cuff muscles. While dancers and gymnasts are in the air they must already be controlling their landings or they will be way off kilter. Tennis players are no different.

How should a tennis player warm up for a match? Theories about proper training techniques in sports have changed so much in the past few years. An interesting study was done at the New York City Marathon a few years back, where physicians checked runners who stretched in their warm-ups before the race and others who did not, to see who would get hurt. The interesting thing is that the runners who had stretched without a previous warm-up had 50 percent more injuries than those who had not. Tennis players should take note of this. Stretching exercises are most important for lightly loosening the muscle-tendon areas. If you really want to loosen the muscles you have to increase your body's flow of blood. This means you have to get your body temperature up, and that means you have to work at it. Break a sweat. If you try to do something explosive and your muscles are not warmed to the occasion, you will pull on them and quite possibly tear them.

Now for the mental side of a warm-up. In muscle physiology there is what is known as a "resting potential." Muscle nerves are constantly sending impulses, but until these impulses go above the body's resting potential, there will be no contraction. Once the impulses rise above it, the muscle will take off. This means that if you are mentally alert, your body's resting potential is much closer to the excitation potential, which means you are that much closer to setting off the muscles. By being mentally alert, you have already added sparks to the system, and in this state very little energy is needed for muscle activity. You cannot achieve quickness if the body and mind are not in concert.

KINETIC REHABILITATION

When a tennis player is injured, Rick Elstein will look at the player's strokes to determine any needed change; he will also study the footwork for injury-causing flaws. With proper drilling and with David Balsley's help, the player can return safely to the court. Balsley explains such kinetic rehabilitation:

For any motion you wish to make, first you must have stabilization of the joint. There are certain muscles in the body that control and stabilize the joint so that you can move it any way you want, at any speed. In balance drills you are working on the control and stabilization of these joints, and once you stabilize a joint, it can move forward, sideways, backward. When you sustain an injury to a joint, stabilization is the first thing you lose because the joint is inflamed. The injury must heal, and then, as the saying goes, you must walk before you can run. We build up the player's muscle and then start him working on wider ranges of motion. The player goes from balancing, say, a right foot, then stepping forward and landing on the leg, then landing sideways. The sheer force of landing sideways is a different force than that of landing straight on and must be exercised. From there the player will move forward and backward, and finally he will practice rotation motions—easily at first, then for speed. Very much the same rehabilitation is used for a victim of tennis elbow. The stabilization of the arm is in the shoulder, and if a player does not learn to stabilize his shoulder, he will hurt himself again when he returns to the court. I would start rehabilitation with a program that first builds up the shoulder, then builds up a moving shoulder, and finish with work on elbow moves. Most tennis elbow sufferers ask extraneous joints to do the work of the shoulder.

Simply put, the most stabilizing joints in the body are the hips and the shoulders. If you are going to move most effectively, you will have to learn to move first from the hips. Your upper body moves should spring from the shoulder. The shoulder is the body's way of connecting the small muscles to the big ones. The hips do the same thing. In tennis you link up your body like a whip—hip to shoulder to racket. If you try to perform the chain of action by skipping some vital link, you are headed for an injury. Tennis Kinetics will keep you honest, and healthy as well.

3 TENNIS EPISODES

Make believe that you have just hit a forehand from the baseline and your opponent is about to return the shot from his baseline. In the time it takes you to read this sentence the ball has gone from your racket to your opponent's and is back to you. That amounts to approximately four seconds. It only took about seven-tenths of one second to stroke the ball. What were you doing with the rest of your time? Whether you're a world-class player or a novice, there is a good chance that you moved. You may not have moved quickly or correctly, but you did not stand still. The *quality* of your movement will determine how well you hit your opponent's return and how well you continue to hit in the point. In the amount of time you've got—about four seconds for groundstrokes, two seconds for volleys—you must perform a sequence of events (photos on pages 34–35):

1. **Reaction.** The ball hitting your opponent's racket is like a gun at the start of a race. *React!* (See photo 1.)

2. **Transition.** You begin to transfer your reaction into *explosive movement.* (See photo 2.)

3. **Movement.** You move to establish a good hitting situation using speed, balance, proper direction, and distance. (See photos 3, 4, and 5.)

4. **Contact.** You hit the ball. If you have performed steps 1, 2, and 3 correctly, you will have a nice shot; if not, you'll be straining for control. (See photo 6.)

. . . . TENNIS EPISODES

33

5. **Recovery.** You are not finished! The ball is still in play. Build good court positioning for the next shot. (See photos 7 and 8.)

6. **Reposition.** Situate yourself on the court so that you can best cover the next ball. Your opponent is about to hit the next ball—the start of a new race. The gun is about to go off. (See photos 9 and 10.)

We call this series of movements a *Tennis Episode*. Each ball you strike requires a Tennis Episode, and each point you play links one Tennis Episode to another. In your own present game you are performing your own version of the Tennis Episode. It may be missing a few steps, or it may follow a different sequence. You may even be playing each shot differently, treating each ball with fresh and untested responses.

We want to show you why our Tennis Episode is the easiest and most efficient method of play. It is designed to be learned quickly and to be retained in your muscle memory. And it is based on the assumption that you do not have to be an expert to be a good player.

We will now analyze each element of the Tennis Episode.

REACTION
. . . .

Imagine that you are about to begin a race—any kind of race. You are primed and ready, and your mind is focused on only one thing—the crack of the starting pistol. Even in long-distance races in which immediate speed is unnecessary, there is a special excitement and intensity of the senses as the racers await the start.

These mental and physical preparations are needed in tennis as much as in running races. The signal you await in tennis is not the sound of the pistol, but the sight of the ball off your opponent's racket. By watching the ball approach his racket, you know when the race is to begin, so you can anticipate its start—a bonus in tennis. But until contact is made you do not know where the ball is going. By assuming a strong Ready Position, your body will be balanced and poised for any race to the ball. Most such tennis "races" amount to quick sprints—usually ten to twenty feet. Think how important a clean start is for these races.

1

2

3

Reaction . . . Transition . . . Movement . . .
Contact . . . begin Recovery,
maintaining balance . . . Recovery . . .
Repositioning . . . Getting into a
new Ready Position.

6

7

4

5

8

9

10

BASIC TENNIS KINETICS. . . . .

36

Common Errors of Reaction

Purely physical errors in this important first phase of the Tennis Episode will retard your reactions and delay the remainder of the Episode, and they can produce a poor kinetic chain for your shot. Physically unprepared positions include straight legs, bending over at the waist, body weight on the heels instead of the balls of the feet, and facing sideways instead of dead-on to the ball. Review the proper Ready Position (see photo this page) and absorb the look of a prepared player.

Mental guessing is the second most common error and is directly linked to the first. The mind and body must work together, and if the body is not ready to move quickly, the mind is the first to know. Often enough the solution is to guess where the ball is going. The guesser will pick a very specific possibility from many possible occurrences. If his guess isn't exactly right, he will probably make an error. Do not guess—*react*.

The third most common error occurs in the course of a rally when a player continues to move toward the center of the court even as his opponent is making contact with the ball. Scrambling back for court position is not nearly as important at this moment as a good reaction to the ball off your opponent's racket. Unless you are way out of court position at the moment your opponent hits his shot, assume a good Ready Position and go from there.

Ready Position: Knees are slightly bent, back is straight, weight is forward on the balls of your feet, racket and hands are in front of your body, midway between the shoulders.

TRANSITION
. . . .

The Transition phase of the Tennis Episode transfers the primed, ready body into movement. This vital Reaction-Transition sequence often determines whether or not you have the time to perform a solid kinetic chain. By beginning the rotation of the hips, shoulders, and torso, you are moving your center of gravity into a good hitting relationship with the oncoming ball.

Transition Highlights

THE VOLLEY

1. Hips and shoulders rotate slightly toward the ball.

2. Racket hand prepares racket upward and forward.

3. Foot nearest the ball pivots toward point of contact.

4. Hips and shoulders begin movement toward point of contact.

Transition: forehand volley.

Transition: backhand volley.

THE OVERHEAD

1. Hips and shoulders rotate to forehand side.

2. Foot on forehand side begins to move away from net.

3. Prepare the racket, moving upward and backward in sync with shoulder rotation.

4. Begin center-of-gravity movement away from the net.

Transition: overhead.

APPROACH SHOT

Hips, shoulders, and racket begin a slight turn toward the anticipated point of contact.

Transition: forehand approach shot.

GROUNDSTROKES

1. Hips and shoulders rotate toward the point of contact.

2. Body weight shifts toward the point of contact.

3. Foot nearest point of contact pivots.

4. Begin racket preparation along with shoulder rotation.

Transition: forehand groundstroke.

Transition: backhand groundstroke.

BALLS HIT DIRECTLY AT YOU

Your transition is the same as for the backward movement of the overhead, except the preparation of the racket is lower.

RETURN OF SERVE

Use the same transition as is used for the volley and ground-stroke.

THE SERVE

1. Weight starts to move forward.

2. Hips and shoulders begin rotation.

3. Movement of hands is down, staying together until the low point of the arc.

4. Attention is focused on balance.

Transition: serve.

Common Errors of Transition

There are three basic errors at the Transition phase: one in body work, another in footwork, and the third in racket preparation. Many players fail to begin the rotation of hips and shoulders in this phase, which delays the body turn. The footwork error is made when movement is initiated with a sideskip; the skip delays or eliminates the hip/shoulder rotation and reduces coverable distance on the court. In racket preparation, many players swing the arm back rather than allow the rotation of the hips and shoulders to prepare the racket. This leads to a longer than necessary back-swing, which, as mentioned in chapter 2, can cause many problems.

VOLLEY ERRORS

Sidestepping, or no step at all.

Volley error: sideskip volley.

. . . . TENNIS EPISODES

43

OVERHEAD ERRORS

Many players backstep while facing forward, failing to get behind the ball.

GROUNDSTROKE ERRORS

There is no body rotation to prepare for the kinetic chain. A player initiates movement by stepping with the foot nearest the ball, inhibiting rotation and reducing distance. With the ball hit directly at him, a player steps backward without a turn, just as in the overhead error.

APPROACH SHOT ERRORS

The player turns his shoulders too much, catching the ball behind him.

RETURN-OF-SERVE ERRORS

The errors described for groundstroke and the volley movements are applicable to service returns.

Return-of-serve error: sideskip.

SERVICE ERRORS

The attention, visual or mental, is focused on the target court rather than on your movement and rhythm.

MOVEMENT
. . . .

Through proper movement we continue our smooth preparation for the kinetic chain of the stroke, positioning ourselves for perfect ball contact. In the same fashion as the professionals, we move to the optimum hitting area for any ball. This kind of accuracy of movement demands control, balance, and timing. While you are moving, the flight of the oncoming ball is yielding valuable information: height over the net, the nature of the ball's spin, pace, and direction. The ball's final signature is its bounce on your side of the net; being highly attuned to that moment, you will have received all the information you need to make the right moves to the ball.

Powerful body movement requires a lowering of the body's center of gravity. This is done through the hips and legs. Your knees should be bent for quick starts, for balance while changing direction, and as shock absorbers for stopping. Keep your back straight. Bending at the waist does not lower your center of gravity; it merely affords you a closer look at local ant life. Good posture counts on the tennis court. It will give you a level field of vision, which will aid you in judging the ball. Finally, balance the weight of your body on the balls of your feet to improve quickness and agility.

. . . . **TENNIS EPISODES**

45

Movement Highlights

VOLLEY

1. Cross-step with the foot farther from the point of contact; if the ball is to your left, cross-step with the right foot.

2. Shoulders and hips rotate forward toward the point of contact, guiding the racket into the area for contact. Racket starts to move forward, from above the ball, toward firm contact with the ball.

Movement: backhand volley.

VOLLEYS HIT AT YOU

1. Step forward with the foot used for a backhand volley.

2. Reach forward with the racket to meet the ball well in front.

3. Go to the ball—don't wait for it to arrive.

Movement: volley, ball hit at you.

. . . . TENNIS EPISODES

47

OVERHEAD

1. The hips, torso, and shoulders complete the turn to the forehand side. The first step back is taken by the foot on the same side as the forehand. Follow with running steps toward the baseline, keeping the ball to the forehand side.

2. The racket moves into the proper position above the shoulder.

3. Head and eyes remain up and focused on the ball, especially as it reaches its highest point.

Movement: overhead.

BASIC TENNIS KINETICS. . . . .

48

GROUNDSTROKES

1. Your first step is similar to the one you use for the volley cross-step (but don't lunge), and is extremely important for maximum court coverage, for getting your center of gravity moving in the direction of contact, and for facilitating hip rotation. Players often take huge, ungainly steps or quick, little baby steps to the ball, thinking that is the quickest way to get someplace. Do not alter the machinery of your footwork so dramatically. Keep the steps as smooth as possible.

2. As the first step is completed, the pivot foot pushes off, propelling the body toward the point of contact.

3. The hips, shoulders, and racket continue to complete their rotation.

4. The final step initiates contact with the ball. Body weight shifts forward as movement ends and the kinetic chain for hitting begins.

Movement: forehand ground-stroke.

. . . . TENNIS EPISODES

49

GROUNDSTROKES HIT AT YOU

1. When groundstrokes are hit deep, the footwork is the same as that used for the overhead.

2. Hips, shoulders, and torso rotate, preparing the racket and body.

3. When groundstrokes are hit short and at you, use the movement of the approach shot.

4. When a ball is near enough to you for only a one-step move, use the movement of a volley—immediate preparation of the hips, shoulders, and racket.

Movement: groundstroke, ball hit at you (the cross-step is used to move forward quickly).

Movement: approach shot.

APPROACH SHOTS

1. Move forward quickly!

2. Hips, torso, and shoulders face the anticipated contact point.

3. The ball is in front of you and slightly to the side, so less shoulder/hip turn is required.

4. Complete a shortened backswing before the final step.

5. Direction of movement should be straight toward the ball.

6. Control your movement through contact. Do not stop. Go directly to the net.

RETURN OF SERVE

1. Hips and shoulders prepare the racket, from either side.

2. Complete a shortened backswing.

3. Eyes and attention are focused on the ball.

4. The footwork for the one-step groundstroke is used.

5. The kinetic chain begins by rotating torso and shoulders forward toward the contact point.

6. For hard and deep serves, the hip and shoulder turns continue from Transition.

7. Treat soft and short serves as you would an approach shot.

8. For serves hit at you, the direction of movement is toward the center of the court; this ensures good court positioning.

. . . . **TENNIS EPISODES**

51

SERVE

1. The hands separate.

2. The tossing arm moves upward, with the racket moving in a full arc up and back.

3. The arms move up in unison.

4. The hips and shoulders continue their rotation.

5. After completing the rotation, the hips stop and reverse direction.

Movement: serve.

1   2   3

Common Movement Errors

Probably the most fundamental movement error is to use different footwork—skipping to nearby balls or taking long strides, short strides, and combinations of both. It can cause a multitude of problems.

- It can lead you to lose your balance.

- It shortens the amount of court you can cover. You will be cutting off far fewer angles and will be getting passed far more frequently.

- It delays your hip/shoulder turn. Without the hip/shoulder turn there is no power, limiting your selection of shots and control.

- It promotes backward movement. This means that your center of gravity is moving the wrong way, your weight is on the wrong foot, and your shoulder turn is delayed. You may be forced to pop the ball into the air.

- It takes time away from the rest of the Tennis Episode.

Another big movement error is "circling the ball" (running backward and behind the ball). This is done by a lot of players who are trying to steal a little bit of time for extra preparation. The bad news is that this doesn't work. If an oncoming ball is traveling at fifty miles an hour and the player is not moving forward to cut it off, he's in big trouble. A player can only move at about one-tenth the speed of the ball. In trying to outrun the ball he will only minimize his chances for a good play.

Here are other, more specific movement errors for the various strokes:

VOLLEYS

- Lack of a cross-step.

- Racket is too far behind the body and too low.

OVERHEAD

- Backpedaling rather than turning and running.

- Poor rotation of shoulders and hips.

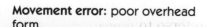

Movement error: poor overhead form.

. . . . TENNIS EPISODES

53

Movement error: poor form during groundstroke. Take the bend out of your waist and put it in your knees.

GROUNDSTROKES

- Sideskipping.

- Standing upright during movement.

- Using different footwork patterns.

- Circling the ball instead of moving directly to the point of contact.

- Poor body rotation.

SHOTS HIT DIRECTLY AT YOU

- Backpedaling without turning the torso to prepare racket and body for contact.

APPROACH SHOTS

- Lack of aggressiveness in getting to the ball.

- Stopping to hit the ball.

RETURN OF SERVE

- Poor preparation of hips and shoulders.

- Moving sideways rather than forward.

- Sideskipping.

SERVE

- The hands move separately (out of sync) instead of together.

- Poor body rotation.

- Racket preparation is too late or too slow.

- Not attending to the ball.

BASIC TENNIS KINETICS . . . .

54

CONTACT

We call the ideal point of contact on eact shot the *Strike Zone*. For example, on a forehand groundstroke the Strike Zone is waist-high and slightly in front of the forward foot, with elbows slightly bent. The racket travels from low to high with a square racket face, and the shot is executed with the fundamentals of a good stroke. On a forehand approach shot the Strike Zone changes. The closer you get to the net area, the higher your point of contact. The Strike Zone for an approach shot should be somewhere between the waist and the shoulder, depending on your proximity to the net. For a volley, the Strike Zone is higher.

If you have performed the Reaction, Transition, and Movement elements of the Tennis Episode well, the Contact element follows naturally.

Contact Highlights

VOLLEY

1. The kinetic chain—hips, shoulders, and racket rotate into contact.

2. The Strike Zone is shoulder height.

3. If the ball is low, adjust your body to it, lowering your center of gravity by bending the knees.

4. Short follow-through.

Contact: volley.

. . . . TENNIS EPISODES

55

OVERHEAD

1. Unwind the hips, torso, and shoulders, powering the racket up into contact with the ball.

2. The Strike Zone height requires full extension of the racket arm above the body.

3. Contact is in front of the body and in front of the racket shoulder. Complete the full arc of the swing with a continuing rotation of the shoulder and arm.

Contact: overhead.

GROUNDSTROKES

1. The classic kinetic chain is used in the groundstrokes.

2. The Strike Zone height for the forehand and backhand is waist level, forward of the front foot.

3. Distance of contact from the body should accommodate a slight flex in the elbow.

Contact: forehand. At moment of contact, slightly drag the big toe of the rear foot to aid stability as the ball leaves the racket.

. . . . TENNIS EPISODES

57

APPROACH SHOTS

1. Continue forward movement through contact, maintaining balance and momentum.

2. The moment of contact often occurs between steps, especially on the forehand.

3. The Strike Zone height is between chest and waist level, preferably high and well forward of the body.

4. Distance from contact should accommodate a slight flex in the elbow.

5. The follow-through continues the racket movement toward the target.

Contact: approach shot.

BASIC TENNIS KINETICS. . . . .

58

RETURN OF SERVE

1. For hard and deep serves, use the Strike Zone for the volley or groundstroke.

2. On soft, short serves, use the Strike Zone for approach shots.

3. For serves in between, use the Strike Zone for groundstrokes.

SERVE

1. The kinetic chain described for pitching a baseball is used: transferring from the hips, through the trunk, the shoulders, racket arm, and wrist.

2. The Strike Zone height is a full reach with the ball placed in front of the shoulder.

Contact: *serve.*

Common Contact Errors

If you find yourself having problems with control of the ball, this would be a good time for a quick review of the discussion in chapter 2 of what effect the impact of the ball can have on your ability to control the racket. If the impact of the ball is not your problem, more than likely it is the location of impact—where, in relation to your body, you are meeting the ball. You may be allowing the ball to drop too low, or you may be hitting too late or too close to your body—anywhere but in the Strike Zone.

VOLLEY ERRORS

- Strike Zone is off—usually the player is late or lets the ball drop.
- A late forward shift of weight.

OVERHEAD ERRORS

- As a result of poor movement, the ball is too far behind.
- As a result of poor body rotation, there is no kinetic chain, no power.

GROUNDSTROKE ERRORS

- The Strike Zone is ignored.
- Poor body preparation and absence of rotation destroys the kinetic chain, especially on groundstrokes hit directly at you, resulting in poor racket control.

RECOVERY

The purpose of the Recovery phase is to change the direction of your movement back toward a good court position. Recovery allows you to complete your shot cleanly and get a good start on the next ball. The beginning of Recovery is characterized by the same explosiveness as your initial reaction to the opponent's ball, and usually it involves a change in direction.

In your first step, the body's momentum is brought under control and is redirected toward the proper court position. This step is followed by vigorous sidestepping similar to the position used by basketball players on defense: shoulders and torso face forward, hands and racket are up and forward, eyes and attention are focused on the flight of the ball. This combines quickness with a good Ready Position from which to react.

Recovery Highlights

THE VOLLEY

1. Following Contact, control your movement by catching your balance with your rear foot, then step behind the cross-step foot.

2. Your cross-step foot moves toward the proper court position to defend against the next shot.

3. The second Recovery step is large, powered by an explosive push with the leg closer to the sideline.

4. Recovery ends with your body moving into the Ready Position (knees bent, weight on the balls of the feet, back straight, racket and hands toward the ball).

Recovery: forehand volley.

Recovery: backhand volley.

THE OVERHEAD

1. The forward motion of the follow-through should allow you to move toward the net.

2. Retreat only if you have made contact behind the halfway point between the service and baselines.

3. As you recover, square your body into a "moving" Ready Position and attend to the ball.

APPROACH SHOT

1. Following Contact, accelerate forward to gain the correct position on court at the net.

2. As you run forward, keep your racket above waist level, with body, eyes, and attention oriented toward the ball.

Recovery: overhead.

Recovery: approach shot.

Recovery for backhand: groundstroke.

GROUNDSTROKES

1. With your back foot, step behind and to the outside of the front foot.

2. Push hard out of this step into a sidestep, maintaining good Ready Position.

3. Eyes and attention are focused on the ball.

RETURN OF SERVE

1. For hard, deep serves, the Recovery is the same as that used for the volley—a balance step followed by sidesteps directed toward the proper court position.

2. For short and soft serves, which bring you forward, use the maneuvers of the approach shot—controlled but continuous movement forward following Contact, toward the proper net position.

3. For serves hit at you, try to maneuver your body into position so that you will hit the ball while moving toward center court.

4. For serves where groundstrokes are appropriate, use the Recovery for groundstrokes.

THE SERVE

1. Catch your balance and regain the Ready Position.

2. For serve-and-volley, Recovery means regaining your balance.

Recovery: serve.

Common Errors of Recovery

There are three very common errors in the Recovery phase.

First, there is no positive movement. The player, having just hit the ball, will stand and watch it fly instead of recovering for the next ball.

Second, the player runs back to the corner of the court instead of sideskipping his way back. Recovery is when you *should* side-skip.

Third, the player is not focusing his attention on the ball before it makes contact with his opponent's racket. Remember, this is your starting gun for the race to the next shot.

As far as technique is concerned, there is a tendency to use the front foot to stop the body's momentum after contact. This causes the body weight to fall back and pulls you off your shot. As for sideskipping, the only time you don't use it is when you have been pulled so far off the court that you must run to get back into play.

The most common error of all is running through the shot. The player uses no braking action after contact and loses his balance and control. That error usually spawns another. In his efforts to avoid a "runaway shot," the player will not even complete the stroke. He will instead pull the weight off his lead foot on contact and transfer it to the other, hoping not to lose court positioning. The correct method is a lot easier and tends to get better results.

REPOSITIONING FOR THE NEXT SHOT
. . . .

Think of Repositioning as the link between runners in a relay race. For a brief instant during the passing of the baton the racers are one; they join at the end of one race and the beginning of the next. The quality of one runner's finish produces an advantage or disadvantage for the next runner. That is the purpose of Repositioning—*to create an advantage in court position and to transfer that advantage to the next Tennis Episode.*

To accomplish a smooth and successful transfer of rhythm the player must do three things well:

• He must assume the correct body position in order to react efficiently and effectively.

• He must prepare mentally for another race to begin.

• He must be accurate in gaining a good court position.

. . . . TENNIS EPISODES

65

The attitude must be one of preparation for a second race—primed, poised, and ready for the gun to sound again. You know how a race begins: Ready, . . . Set, . . .

In tennis, the proper ready and set positions mean that:

- Hips, torso, and shoulders are facing the opponent and the anticipated ball/racket contact.

- The racket is centered between the shoulders and above the waist.

- The player continues his sideways movement until the instant before the ball makes contact.

- At that instant the final body movement is a small hop on the balls of the feet a split second prior to your opponent's impact. Your timing puts both feet on the court at the moment the ball makes contact with your opponent's racket. The sounds of your feet hitting the court and the ball hitting the strings of your opponent's racket should be one.

Repositioning: the Split Step—connecting the repositioning element to the Ready Position for the next shot.

1 2 3

Common Repositioning Errors

The most common technical error during Repositioning is to drop the racket head. Keep it up and in the center of your body. One of the larger problems in tennis is knowing where to be on the court, and by trying to reposition while your opponent is making contact you only complicate your situation. If you have committed yourself to one side of the court and are stuck there, it is far better to concede the middle ground, stop where you are, and play the ball as best you can. Even though you may not be in the best court position, you *must* be mentally ready to play the ball. *It is more important to have good body position than it is to achieve good court position.* Even the best players find themselves in awkward court positions, but it is extremely rare to see them react with awkward body movement. When an opponent sees that your body is still in a strong Ready Position, he will probably not try to hit the ball behind you and instead will play the ball to the open court, giving you a chance. Though you may be in a compromising position, you will still have forced your opponent to play the ball the way you want him to play it.

Positioning Maps

The following positioning maps are your key to efficient coverage. Proper court position is determined by the location of your shot on your opponent's side and by your location in the forecourt or backcourt. In order to cover the court properly, you must position yourself in the center of the angle formed by the two possible returns farthest away from you that are available to your opponent. Many players, not realizing the geometric sense of this, try to dash back to the center of the court. Remember, the court's center mark is rarely the best place to be for your opponent's next shot. The maps show you the optimum places to wait for the ball.

By positioning yourself according to the placement of your shots, you can gain a step or two and lay preparation for your next Tennis Episode. With practice you will find yourself adjusting automatically to the shots you play. After a few weeks of drilling you should notice a more focused attention on the ball, quicker reactions to an opponent's shots, and a lot more time to execute shots of your own.

. . . . TENNIS EPISODES

67

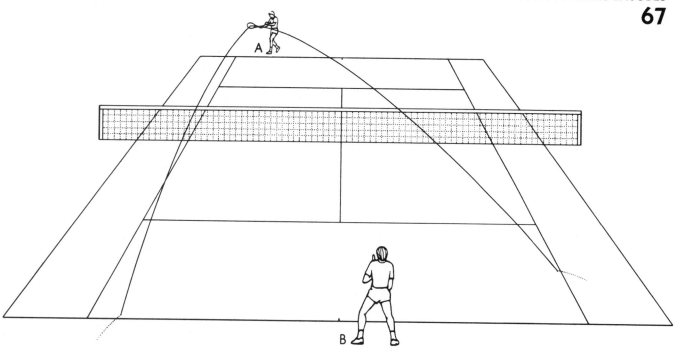

Balls hit to the deuce corner require you (B) to position slightly to the right side of the center mark and behind the baseline.

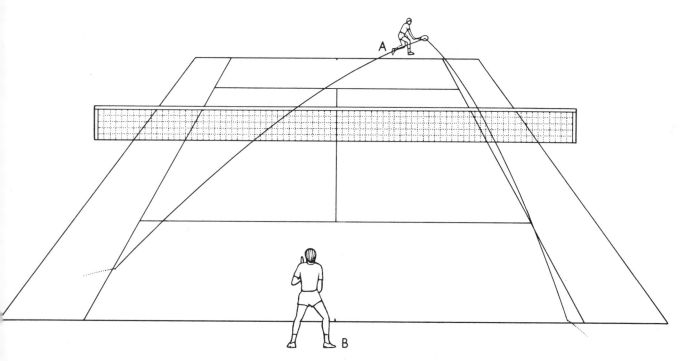

Balls hit to the ad corner require B to position slightly to the left side of the center mark and behind the baseline.

BASIC TENNIS KINETICS. . . . .

68

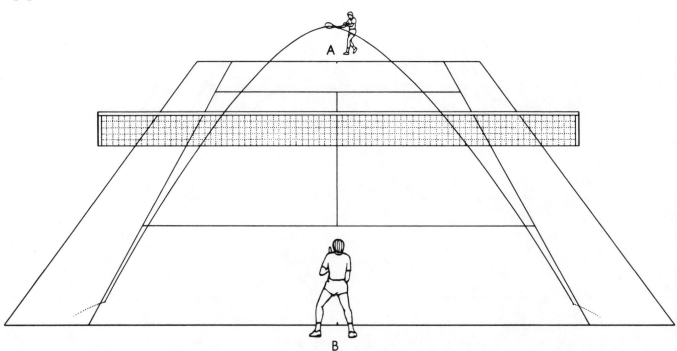

Balls hit to the center of the court require a court position behind the center mark and baseline.

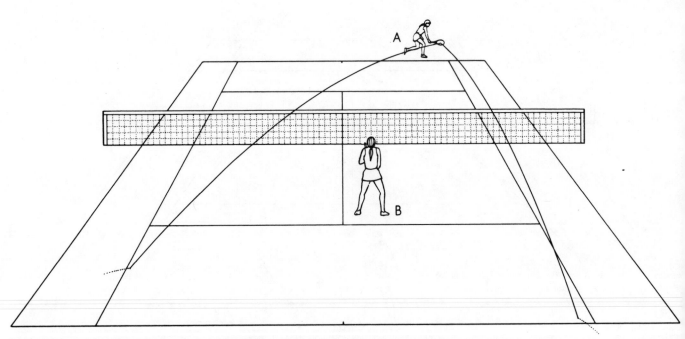

At net, balls landing in the ad corner require B to position slightly to the same side of the center line as the bounce of the ball.

. . . . TENNIS EPISODES

69

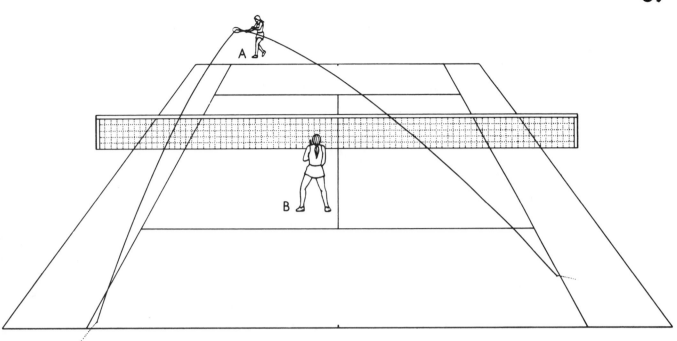

Balls landing in the deuce corner require B to position on the same side of the center line as the bounce of the ball.

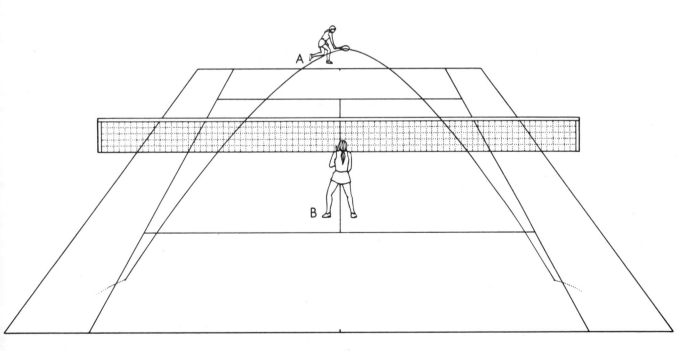

Balls landing in the center require B to straddle the center line.

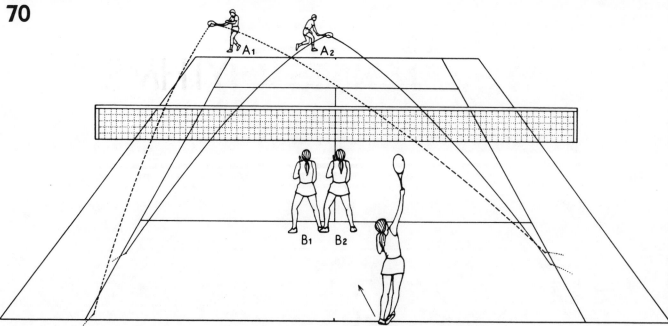

Serves hit to the deuce service box: For a serve hit to the wide side (A1), a split-step position (B1) is required—slightly to the same side of the "T" (where the center line and the service lines meet). For a serve placed down the center (A2), position B2 behind the "T" is required.

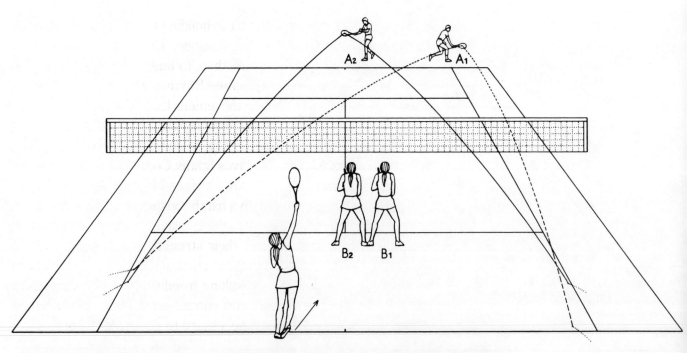

Serves to the ad service box: The split-step positions for serves to the wide and center positions of the ad service box are illustrated. Their locations are guided by the same principle as for the deuce service box.

4 TENNIS RHYTHMS

In chapter 3 we gave you the basic building blocks of your game—the five elements of the Tennis Episode. But what is the mortar used to connect one brick to another, to build a strong and unified structure? The answer is *rhythm*. Rhythm is a flow—a flow of motion whereby one balanced movement leads to another. As this flow develops, it produces its own momentum, and the rhythm gets stronger, making movement more consistent, more harmonious, more powerful. Rhythm gives Jimmy Connors the power to hit ten screaming backhands in a row; it gives Martina the flexibility of going from a soft-paced dink to a harsh topspin winner. While most players weaken as rallies lengthen, players like Connors and Navratilova get stronger, and their strength lies in the power of their basic rhythms. Through these rhythms your Tennis Episodes become automatic, and the resulting freedom from thinking about stroking details allows you to concentrate on the ball. This chapter shows you the basic rhythms necessary to play sound tennis.

BASIC TENNIS KINETICS . . . .

72

THE VOLLEY
. . . .

Is there anything more embarrassing and deflating than being passed cold at the net? Every player has felt the sting of passing shots, and the very thought of getting passed discourages many players from exercising their net-playing options. The cold beauty of the volley is that it can be the simplest of shots if done correctly

The forehand volley: Ready Position . . . Turn hips and shoulders . . . Complete cross-step and Contact . . . Balance and begin Recovery step . . . Recovery and Reposition toward the center . . . Split step into a new Ready Position.

1   2   3

and the most exasperating if done poorly. In the half second it takes for most volleys, it is astounding how much can go wrong.

So do it right. The key to the volley is in the Reaction-Transition-Movement sequence contained in the cross-step. With one move you accomplish the first four elements of a high-grade Tennis Episode, all in correct order, all very quickly and efficiently.

4   5   6

Split step into Ready Position.

1

2

The backhand volley: Turn hips and shoulders . . . Complete cross-step and Contact . . . Balance and begin Recovery step . . . Recovery and Reposition toward the center . . . Split-step into a new Ready Position.

3   4   5

BASIC TENNIS KINETICS. . . . .

76

OVERHEADS

. . . .

For many tennis players faced with the prospect of hitting an overhead, the usual reaction is to become an observer and hope the ball will go out. For others the smash is a reward for good approach shots and volleys, and a chance to end the point in fine style.

Keep the ball between yourself and the net. If the ball travels behind you, turn and run back; don't sidestep or backpedal.

1

2

3

. . . . **TENNIS RHYTHMS**

77

The overhead: Ready . . . Hips and shoulders turn, complete backstep, begin racket preparation . . . Continue Movement with a cross-step . . . Balance on the third step, stay sideways . . . Unwind kinetic chain into Contact, switching position of feet . . . Run forward, end with a split step for a new Ready Position.

4   5   6

BASIC TENNIS KINETICS . . . .

78

Backhand Overheads

Through poor court position on our part, or fine shots on theirs, good opponents will find a way to make us play lobs from the backhand side. This calls for a backhand overhead. The objective is the same as for all overheads: get behind the ball. Turning and running to the backhand side requires the same technique as for a forehand overhead. Getting the shoulders turned and the racket

The backhand overhead: Ready Position . . . Hips and shoulders turn . . . Complete cross-step moving away from the net. (Note that movement is to the side. The backhand overhead is used *only* when a regular overhead is not possible, so if you can go straight back, use the regular overhead.) . . . Continue moving backward, continue to turn shoulders . . . Reverse shoulder rotation (kinetic chain) into contact.

1   2   3

· TENNIS RHYTHMS

79

into a hitting position early are critical. There's little chance of generating overpowering pace, but whatever power you do create will be executed by trying to produce a kinetic chain. Rotate your shoulders toward the net, trying to punch the ball deep down the line; attempting a short crosscourt angle is almost hopeless. And wherever your shot lands, remember to recover properly.

4   5

APPROACH SHOTS
. . . .

The approach shot: From the Ready Position, move directly toward the ball . . . Use a short backswing . . . Fit the Contact of the ball *smoothly* into your movement . . . After Contact, accelerate once more toward the net.

The approach shot is just what you've been waiting to use, and now you can. Here comes a short ball. The approach is made while moving forward to seize the offensive, so take charge of this moment at once and with authority.

To be successful with your approach you should:

1. Use controlled and continuous movement in your charge toward the net.

2. Focus on placing the ball deep in your opponent's court without overplaying the ball.

3. Direct most approach shots deep down the lines.

4. Remember that the approach is only one shot in an offensive play. It is not designed to be an outright winner, though sometimes it might be one.

3

4

GROUNDSTROKES

No matter what type of game you tend to play, the meat and potatoes of tennis is in the groundstrokes.

The early part of the groundstroke rhythm is meant to get your body into position to produce a solid kinetic chain.

1

2

The forehand groundstroke: Ready Position . . . Turn hips
and shoulders . . . Complete cross-step, continuing turn and
racket preparation . . . Continue moving, step with back foot

3

4

. . . Step with front foot . . . Shift weight to front foot on making Contact; *hold your balance with a slight drag of the toe of the back foot* . . . Recover with back foot . . . Sideskip back to Ready Position.

6

7

8

1   2   3

The backhand groundstroke: Ready Position . . . Turn hips and shoulders . . . Complete cross-step, continuing turn and racket preparation . . . Continue moving, step with back foot . . . Step with front foot . . . Weight shifts to front foot making contact . . . *Maintain balance with slight drag of the toe of the back foot . . .* Recover with back foot . . . Sideskip back to Ready Position.

4

5

7

8

9

Groundstroke Variations

THE BACKSTEP

A form of backward movement is needed to handle balls hit directly at the body on the baseline. The footwork is the same as that used for the overhead. And just as with the smash, movement of the torso and racket, and the backstep, occur first, immediately followed by running steps. The angle of your backward movement should afford you the chance to play the ball in your normal Strike Zone.

1

2

The backstep variation for groundstrokes: Turn hips and shoulders early. Use the cross-step to go forward quickly . . . Stop and step into contact of the ball.

3

THE ONE-STEP

Sometimes the ball will bounce close enough to you to necessitate only one step; appropriately enough, we call this the one-step. Simply put, you make your turn, backswing, and contact all with one step. Time is often short in this situation, so be sure to have the proper Ready Position. Without a balanced body you will not be able to control the torso in time to control your racket.

One-step variation for groundstrokes.   1   2

3

4

The Return of Serve
. . . .

When you consider that the only way to win a match is by breaking the serve of your opponent, you can see how critical it is to implement a rhythmic return of serve. The shot is almost always performed under pressure and, particularly against a strong server, you are in a position of weakness right at the start. By establishing strong rhythms against any serve you may face, you will add a new dimension to both your offensive and defensive games.

VERSUS HARD AND DEEP SERVES

1. First, and most important, turn the hips and shoulders, and if time permits, combine two basic rhythms—the cross-step of the volley for Reaction, Transition, and Movement, and the hip-and-shoulder turn and racket preparation for the ground-strokes.

The return of serve: Ready Position . . . Hips and shoulders turn first . . . Racket is prepared . . . (Notice Martina does not use the cross-step here—time does not permit it.)

1

2

2. The Recovery steps are those of the volley, with quickness especially important if your opponent's game is serve-and-volley.

VERSUS SOFT AND SHORT SERVES

These types of serves require the response of an approach shot.

VERSUS OTHER SERVES

The spin serve and kick serve, among others, usually require the rhythm of a groundstroke.

3

4

BASIC TENNIS KINETICS. . . . .

94

THE SERVE

. . . .

The serve is the only stroke in the game that does not require running, so the server gets to decide when and where to hit the ball. The success of one's serve depends on the ability to produce a high-quality kinetic chain, as in any of the other strokes, and to coordinate movements with the toss of the ball. The forces of the ball on the racket at impact are present in the serve as they are on the other strokes, and the kinetic chain is important for both power and accuracy.

By developing an automatic rhythm on your serve, you can concentrate strictly on the ball. The rhythm for the serve is *down-up*—and *hit*.

1

2

3

The serve: Ready Position . . . Arms go down together . . . Arms go up together . . . Legs, hips, and shoulders begin kinetic chain, and racket head drops . . . Contact. Complete kinetic chain . . . Recover.

4   5   6

CONNECTING THE RHYTHMS
. . . .

Continuous rhythm generates kinetic energy for the entire Tennis Episode and charges the next Episode with power and consistency. Great players are able to maintain rhythm and build a reservoir of energy. This is done by infusing the rhythm from the Recovery/ Repositioning elements of one Tennis Episode into the Reaction

1   2   3

Connecting the serve-and-volley: Recovery from serve, Movement toward the net . . . Continued Movement toward the net . . . Split-step to the Ready Position . . . Hips and shoulders turn for backhand volley . . . Cross-step and Contact . . . Recovery step, balance on back foot . . . Reposition toward Ready Position . . . Split step again into Ready Position.

element of the next. The technique for the transfer is the *split step,* as described in the approach shot section. Actually, this step is the key to connecting all rhythms in tennis. It is extremely important to begin each Episode from a good Ready Position, and the split step is the way to do it.

4

5

7

8

9

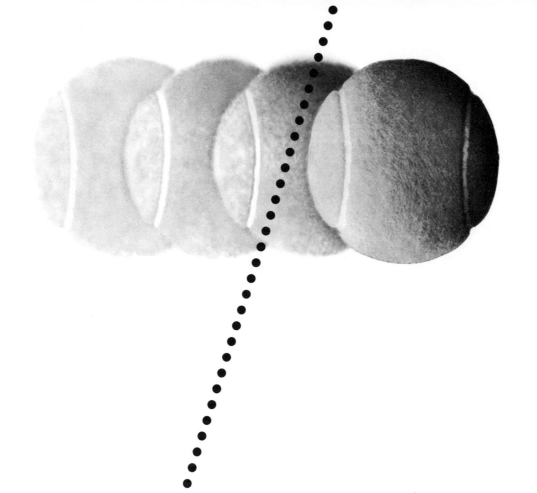

TWO

DEVELOPING YOUR TENNIS KINETICS

5 THE PROGRAM

We are now going to present a Tennis Kinetics program of development for any type of player. It can be your program whether you're a beginner, intermediate, or of advanced tournament caliber, and it incorporates sound fundamentals of play whether your game is backcourt, net, singles, or doubles.

Here's how the program works. There are nine groups of drills based on the Tennis Episodes you learned in section 1:

1. Groundstrokes

2. Groundstroke Variations

3. Serve

4. Return of Serve

5. Approach Shot

6. Volley

7. Overhead

8. Connecting Tennis Episodes

9. Combinations of Strokes

Each of these groups consists of drills for three levels of play—beginner, intermediate, advanced/tournament—which combine into four cycles for personal development, accelerating the learning process dramatically with concentrated focus on proper technique.

DEVELOPING YOUR TENNIS KINETICS . . . .

102

Cycle 1: Groundstrokes

Develops groundstrokes and groundstroke variations, connections for groundstrokes and combinations of shots used when playing from the backcourt.

Cycle 2: Serve and Return of Serve

Concentrates on the serve and return of serve; also stresses the importance of the shots that follow.

Cycle 3: The Net Game

Works on the complete net game—approach shots, volleys, and overheads—and develops the player's ability to connect these strokes.

Cycle 4: The Serve-and-Volley

Develops both the serve-and-volley player and the player who faces serve-and-volleyers. In this cycle the stress is on technique, timing, and connections between serves, volleys, and overheads for aggressive forecourt play.

HOW TO BEGIN

A. *Read through the drills in each group.* You will find three different types of drills that require another player: feeder drills, partner drills, and competitor drills.

In the feeder drills, one person at first acts as coach to the other, then the two players switch roles. This is a good learning experience for both players, and whether you're a beginner or advanced player, you will benefit from the opportunity to observe in the feeder role. One bit of advice: Since the feeder does not reply to the shots of his practice partner, he will be using a lot of balls during the course of a practice session, so a ball hopper is a recommended purchase.

In the partner drills both participants are practicing, though they may be working on separate techniques. Both players derive benefit from the drills, so each depends on the other to continue the rallies and keep the ball in play. Winners should not be attempted until each player has hit five to ten shots. The partner

. . . . THE PROGRAM

103

drills improve upon and fine-tune the concepts learned in the feeder drills. If you are making too many errors in the partner drills, go back to or try the feeder format. Partner drills are complementary drills; as one player practices serves and groundstrokes, say, the other is returning serves and hitting groundstrokes of his own. Remember to exchange roles on all the drills during each practice session.

In the competitor drills, both participants play to win. Focus on the specific purpose of each drill and execute what has been learned in the feeder and partner drills. If too many errors are being committed, go back to the other drills.

As part of most drill groups, we offer combination drills for you to use should you "lose it" on court. At some time or other every player is faced with a slump. These combination drills will help you to break out of your slump and get back on track.

B. *Based on the drills you have reviewed, determine your level of entry (see headings for each drill group) by estimating your general level of play—beginner, intermediate, or advanced.* Begin with cycle 1, and progress from the groundstroke program through the groundstroke variations, connections, and combinations. Once you have completed the first cycle you may go to any of the others. Beginners should follow the sequence of cycles 1 through 4, completing all the programs and drills before moving on to the next level. Intermediate and advanced/tournament players should consider the following when choosing their appropriate cycles:

1. Work on your weaknesses. If your serve or return of serve costs you matches, use cycle 2. If you are missing smashes or producing weak approach shots, get into cycle 3. If you are fodder for serve-and-volleyers or if the timing of your own serve-and-volley game is off, beef up your game with cycle 4.

2. If you are a singles player without a net game and you wish to become an all-court player, or if you are a doubles specialist, cycle 3 is for you.

3. Work on your best shots or develop some new ones by concentrating on the advanced drills for the strokes you prefer.

DEVELOPING YOUR TENNIS KINETICS . . . .

104

PROGRAM GUIDELINES

1. Begin with the first drill listed under your level of play.

2. Perform the drills on both the forehand and backhand sides.

3. Perform the kinetic chain and rhythm drills a few minutes each day, and continue to use them along with the other drills included in your program. That's the best way to make and keep your movements automatic.

4. When you have achieved 70 percent proficiency in one drill, move on to the next. For example, in the forehand crosscourt drill you may advance when you can get seven out of ten shots effectively crosscourt.

5. Use the competitor drills. These drills mark the beginning of Tennis Kinetics principles in competitive play. They stress proper technique and at the same time prepare the player to apply Tennis Kinetics methods in match-type situations.

6. Move on to the next cycle when all the drills have been completed. If you initially went through the cycle as a beginner, you may also choose to repeat the cycle using intermediate-level drills.

OUTLINE OF DEVELOPMENTAL SYSTEM

Cycle 1: Groundstrokes

1. Groundstroke drills (page 108)

2. Groundstroke variation drills (page 129)

3. Connecting drills for groundstrokes and variations (page 163)

4. Combination drills—groundstroke drill (page 169)

Cycle 2: Serve and Return of Serve

1. Serve drills (page 133)

2. Return-of-serve drills (page 140)

3. Connecting drills (page 163)

4. Combination drills (page 169)

Cycle 3: The Net Game

1. Approach shot drills (page 147)

2. Volley drills (page 152)

3. Overhead drills (page 157)

4. Connecting drills (page 163)

5. Combination drills (page 169)

Cycle 4: Serve and Volley

1. Combination drills—serve and volley (page 169)

2. Return-of-serve drills (page 140)

A BRIEF WORD ON GRIPS

Throughout the course of tennis history the game has been played with a myriad of styles, strokes, and strategies. By now the modern-day player has innumerable standards and precedents upon which to build his own game. The manner in which you grip your racket—even this most rudimentary element of the game—has terrific latitude. Whether you choose a Western, Continental, or Eastern grip, or some derivation of any of the three, the important thing to keep in mind is that the grip should allow for a smooth transfer of power and control.

We recommend general usage of the Eastern grip. It gives high performance from every area of the court, and more specifically it:

- uses a good combination of hand and arm muscles to resist the twisting forces created by impact of the ball;

- is the most versatile of grips—good for groundstrokes, approach shots, returns of serve, and volleys;

- promotes quick and easy grip changes, particularly when moving from the backcourt to the forecourt;

- is a strong grip for shots that elude the player's Strike Zone above shoulder height and below the knee.

If you are a beginner, we suggest that you learn the Eastern grip and use it for groundstrokes, volleys, approach shots, and return of serve.

Eastern forehand grip.

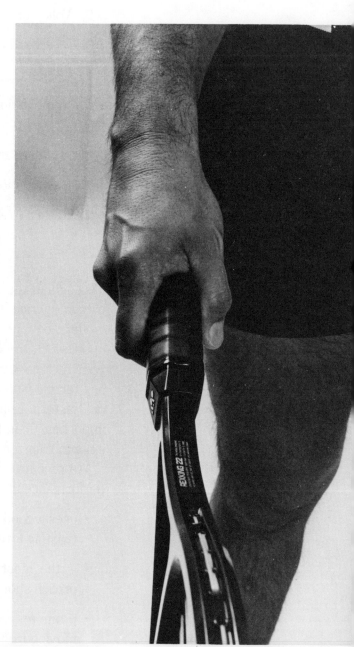

Continental grip.

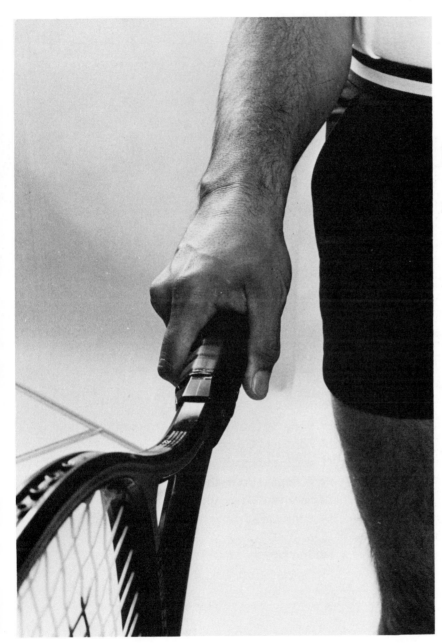

Eastern backhand grip.

6 GROUNDSTROKES

BEGINNER	**1–11**
INTERMEDIATE	**1–13**
ADVANCED	**1–17**

If You "Lose-It" Drills

	GROUNDSTROKES	CONNECTING	COMBINATIONS
Beginner	2–5	1 A only	1 A only
Intermediate	2–5	2	2 A and B
Advanced	4–9, 16, 17	2	2 A and B

DRILL 1

Kinetic Chain

With the help of a full-length mirror, this drill trains you to focus your attention on the movement of your body as you produce a groundstroke. Because no ball is used, the player concentrates solely on his kinetic chain, strengthening the chain with every repetition.

Begin by standing sideways to the mirror. Follow the photo sequence on pages 24–25 and slowly take your body through each step of the kinetic chain. Study each and every movement carefully. Once you feel that your own movements are error-free, close your eyes and repeat the moves, seeing and feeling the motions from within. Upon taking the court, you will find yourself recalling the feel you developed without the ball, and this will help you perform your moves correctly and with consistency on court.

You should begin each day of tennis with a few minutes of mirror drills. As you progress, you should slightly quicken the rotation of the hips and shoulders.

DRILL 2

Kinetic Chain with a Ball

This drill initially requires no partner and can be done by standing either forty feet from a wall or on the baseline of a court. Practice forehand and backhand kinetic chains, tossing the ball in front and to the side of your body, high enough to give you plenty of time for proper body movement. Begin your kinetic chain after the bounce of the ball. The spoken rhythm you wish to establish is "bounce, hit": the ball bounces on the word *bounce* and you make contact on the word *hit*. Focus your attention on proper movement, particularly the rotational movement of the hips. Remain aware of the total chain, from legs to hips to torso, etc.

Once you are making quality strokes and solid contact, control the behavior of the ball so that it passes high over the net (or a net line drawn or visualized on the wall) each time. When you can hit ten to fifteen balls in a row with accuracy and quality, recruit a partner to feed balls from the net, twenty to the forehand side and twenty to the backhand, ten sets of each. The feeds should always be to the player practicing his chains, and there should be time between each shot for proper preparation and execution.

DRILL 3

Rhythm Drill without a Ball
....

Start this drill very slowly, walking through each step of the photos on pages 82–87. Hold each step for a count of three. You may find it difficult to maintain your balance, but it's only by performing these movements at a very slow speed that you develop the balance necessary to perform them at high speed.

Take care to complete every rhythm with good balance, and remember to end each sequence with a strong Ready Position. Practice the following sequences:

1. Alternating groundstrokes—forehand to backhand.
2. Repetition of groundstrokes—forehands, then backhands.

You should gradually increase the pace of the movements, maintaining the even tempo of 1-2-3-Hit-5-6-7-Ready Position. *Never sacrifice the correctness of your movement to increase your speed.*

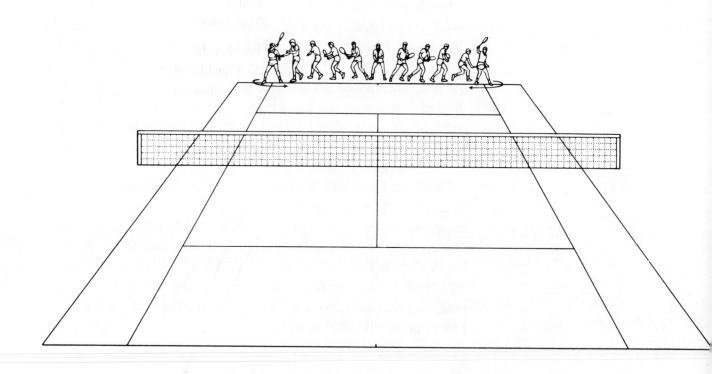

. . . . **GROUNDSTROKES**

111

DRILL 4

Rhythm Drill with a Partner
. . . .

This drill will help you to:

- make your rhythms and movement automatic at higher speeds;

- consistently combine high-quality rhythms, kinetic chains, and points of contact in the Strike Zone;

- control the height, direction, and pace of the ball at various speeds of movement.

Position yourself (B) and your partner (A) as shown in the illustration. Your partner feeds you one ball at a time and your job is to hit each ball directly back to him. Your partner should stretch your abilities by hitting with slightly more pace than you are accustomed to, or by hitting your returns farther and farther from the center of the court. One rule for the partner: Wait until the baseliner has assumed a good Ready Position before feeding the next ball, otherwise the rhythms and chains will break down and balls will be hit out of the Strike Zone.

The following sequences should be used:

1. Alternating forehands and backhands.
2. Repetitions of forehands, then backhands.
3. Random feeding—no particular sequence.

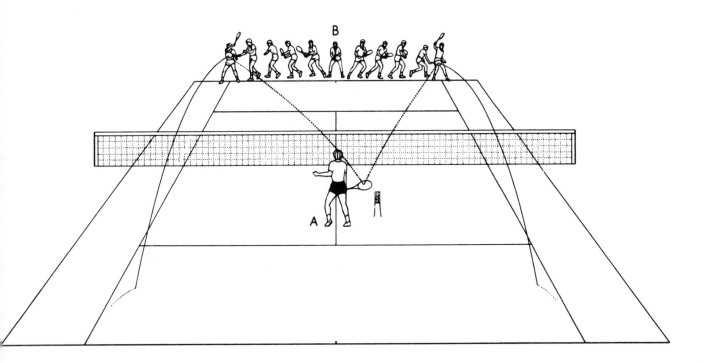

Here's a checklist of techniques that should be mastered before moving on. You should have developed:

- the ability to secure a correct grip as the hips and shoulders begin to turn in the Reaction/Transition phase of each rhythm;

- a smooth, even rhythm of steps during Movement;

- the ability to produce quality kinetic chains combined with Contact of the ball while it is in your Strike Zone;

- the ability to perform a smooth, balanced Recovery step;

- the ability to perform sideskips during Repositioning;

- the technique of ending a rhythm with a good Ready Position with which to begin the next rhythm; and

- the ability to perform all the following sequences of groundstrokes with balance and varied cadences (speeds of movement):
  a. forehand to forehand to forehand
  b. backhand to backhand to backhand
  c. forehand to backhand to forehand
  d. backhand to forehand to backhand

DEVELOPING DEPTH

Let's take a moment off before proceeding to the next drill and talk about depth of groundstrokes. In section 1 of the book we took you through the various kinetic chains of power, analyzed the Tennis Episode, and brought it to life through rhythm. As you develop these basic elements of Tennis Kinetics you will improve your ability to govern the height, speed, spin, and direction of each ball you hit. At this stage of your development, however, the most important characteristic to develop is height of the ball, because height determines depth, and a ball hit with depth is the surest way to create errors and weak returns from an opponent. This can be pretty handy in club-level tennis, where the odds are greater than eight to one that a rally will end in an error! Even in the professional ranks, far more points are won on errors than on winners. So since the last player to hit the ball usually loses the point, it is most important to develop the ability to keep the ball in play and deep into the court.

The effective depth for groundstrokes is within nine feet of the opponent's baseline. All but the most advanced players find this very difficult to achieve, and the reason may surprise you. If you are like most people who fail to achieve consistent depth, you are probably the victim of a powerful optical illusion. Take a look at the diagram below.

It may be hard to believe, but both balls are the same distance from the baseline, even though the ball on the far side of the court appears to be merely inches from being out of bounds. This illusion is constantly at work as you play from the baseline, looking through the net into an apparently shrinking court. For many players, it creates the impression that they are hitting shots desperately close to the baseline when in fact their returns are landing many feet short of the intended mark. On the other hand, a player will often strike a ball *certain* that its height over the net will carry it well out of the court, only to find that it has landed a foot or two inside his opponent's baseline, where it does the most damage. Still gripped by the wonder of his shot's incredible nearness to the baseline (it must have *just* made it!), the player, anxious not to hit the next ball out, will normally follow this terrific shot with an ultrasafe one, and it's back to the minors again. Don't let this happen to you! Now that you are aware of the illusion, counter it.

Just how deceived are you, anyway—how can you tell? The next time you take the court, take this test. Position yourself behind the

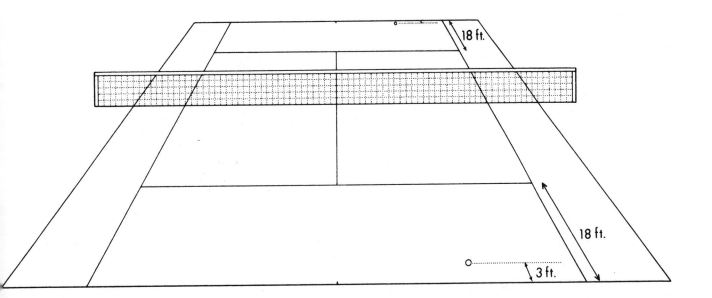

baseline and have a partner take the other side of the court. Your partner feeds you balls, and after each ball you strike, you call out how far from the baseline you believe you hit the ball. After five shots, compare your estimates to the actual distances, as noted by your partner. If you are like most nonprofessionals, your estimates will be off the mark by anywhere from four to six feet—the difference between an effective shot and a weak one.

In tests with over one hundred intermediate, advanced, and professional players, the results have been consistent. Pros can pinpoint their distances to within inches of the actual marks, but most other players are shockingly incorrect, estimating that their groundstrokes bounce within three feet of the baseline when in fact they are six to nine feet short! Approach shot appraisals scored even less acceptable estimations, with players as much as ten feet off on their claims of depth.

You can develop your ability to assess depth accurately by having your partner call out the actual distance from the baseline for each shot you hit. Whether you are a beginner hitting one shot at a time or an advanced player rallying with your partner during a drill, concentrate on watching where the ball has landed, relating that spot to the actual distance called out by your partner. After a while, test yourself by again calling out the distances you estimate for each shot, now with your partner responding yes if correct, or no with the actual distance. This drill can be incorporated into all of the other stroke drills that follow.

DRILL 5

Basic Ball Control to Develop Depth*
. . . .

Place a line of tennis balls across the opposite court, from sideline to sideline and halfway between the service line and the baseline. Your aim is to hit high and deep between the balls and the baseline. The ball should clear the net by five to eight feet. Practice until you are confident of achieving depth into the target area.

Intermediate and advanced players can build power in addition to depth by gradually increasing the speed of the hip/shoulder rotation. Remember, do not swing the arm faster for extra power. Once you have consistently hit the ball within the boundaries of balls and baseline, move the row of balls closer for a tougher target area.

* A ball machine or practice partner is recommended for this drill, but if neither is available the drill can be done alone, in which case you must feed the ball to yourself. To do this, toss the ball high enough in the air that you have time to rotate your hips and shoulders, and in front of you enough so that you can practice the proper Strike Zones for your shots.

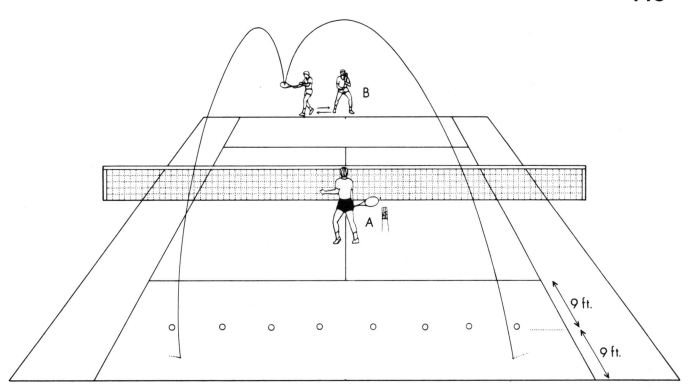

DRILL 6

**Forehand Crosscourt
Groundstrokes**

The purpose of this drill is to develop deep and accurate crosscourt shots by performing the elements of the Tennis Episode for groundstrokes.

FOR THE INTERMEDIATE AND ADVANCED PLAYER

The players are at each baseline as illustrated on the next page. They rally crosscourt to each other, concentrating on combining high-quality rhythms with deep shots (nine feet or less from the baseline). Both players should perform quality Tennis Episodes with each ball struck, which means:

1. A quick Reaction.

2. Turning of the hips and shoulders, and beginning racket preparation.

3. Moving smoothly to the ball.

4. Performing a quality stroke in the Strike Zone.

5. Making a balanced Recovery step.

6. Sideskipping during Repositioning.

7. Assuming a good Ready Position before one's partner hits the next ball.

(Remember that it is more important to be in a strong Ready Position just before your opponent makes contact than it is to continue to move toward the ideal court position; if necessary, sacrifice court position for Ready Position.)

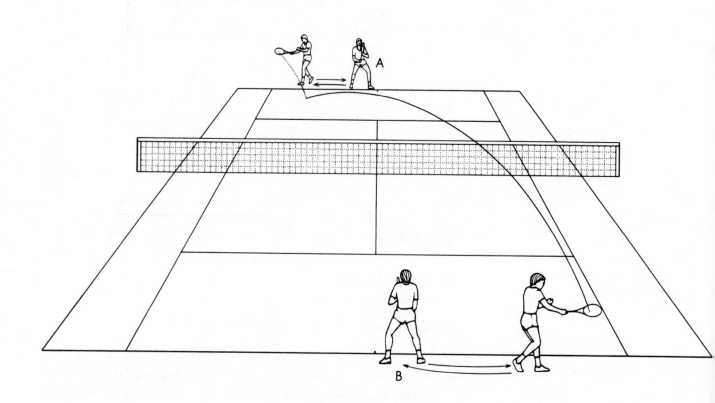

FOR THE BEGINNER

With beginners the crosscourt drill is more effectively practiced when one player positions himself at the net. The net player feeds the ball to the baseline player, then waits for him to assume a good Ready Position near the center of the court before feeding the next ball.

DRILL 7

**Backhand Crosscourt
Groundstrokes**
. . . .

The purpose and directions for this drill are identical to those for the forehand crosscourt drill.

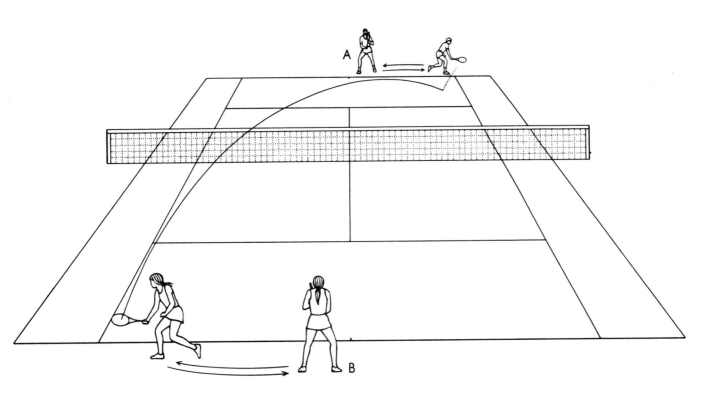

DEVELOPING YOUR TENNIS KINETICS . . . .

118

DRILL 8

Forehand Down-the-Line Groundstrokes

The purpose of this drill is to develop deep and accurate shots down the line while correctly performing the elements of the Tennis Episode for groundstrokes. It is more difficult than the drill for crosscourt groundstrokes, since shots down the line require that a player hit higher and deeper, with a target six feet or less from the baseline. Allow your shots to land well within the sidelines, and upon Recovery reposition close to the center of the court.

FOR THE INTERMEDIATE AND ADVANCED PLAYER

Position as illustrated. Rally in the same manner as in the crosscourt drills, putting emphasis on smooth rhythms and good depth with each stroke.

FOR THE BEGINNER

Proceed as in the crosscourt drills, with one player assuming the net position. Emphasis is on depth and plenty of room from the sidelines on your shots. Do not aim for the lines, but instead develop height and direction, slowly improving your accuracy in hitting down the line.

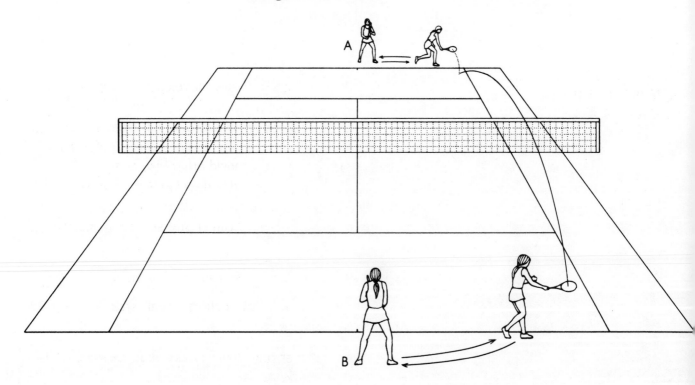

DRILL 9

Backhand Down-the-Line Groundstrokes

The purpose and directions for this drill are identical to those for the forehand drill.

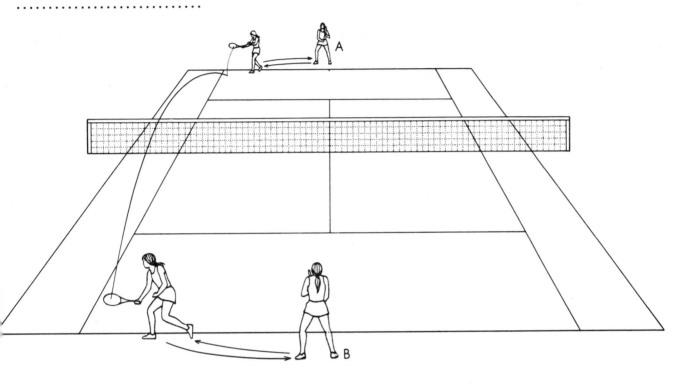

THE WEAK LINK IN GROUNDSTROKES

Tennis players spend many hours developing hard and deep groundstrokes, yet most fail to spend enough time on their weakest link—the high-backhand groundstroke hit from behind the baseline. Without this shot, many intermediate and advanced players lose to opponents they should otherwise beat.

The next two drills are designed to develop better lobbing and to counter the effects of lobs aimed at you. With the introduction of a high, deep lob to a rally, a player can create several point-winning situations:

• He can draw an outright error from his opponent.

• His opponent responds with a short, weak shot, creating an approach shot opportunity.

• His opponent loses strong court positioning, opening up the possibilities for attack.

DRILL 10

Forehand Crosscourt Lob

The purpose of this drill is to develop deep and accurate crosscourt lobs by perfecting the elements of the Tennis Episode.

FOR THE ADVANCED PLAYER

The players rally as in the crosscourt groundstroke drill, Player A hitting groundstrokes while player B hits lobs. The players then switch roles.

FOR THE INTERMEDIATE PLAYER

The players rally as in the crosscourt groundstroke drill, both hitting lobs.

FOR THE BEGINNER

The players perform this drill in the same way as the crosscourt drill for beginners: The feeder is at the net and the other player (the lobber) is at the baseline. Try to:

• be energetic in Recovery; if possible, reposition before your lob lands in your opponent's court; and

• whenever possible, reply to lobs from the Strike Zone.

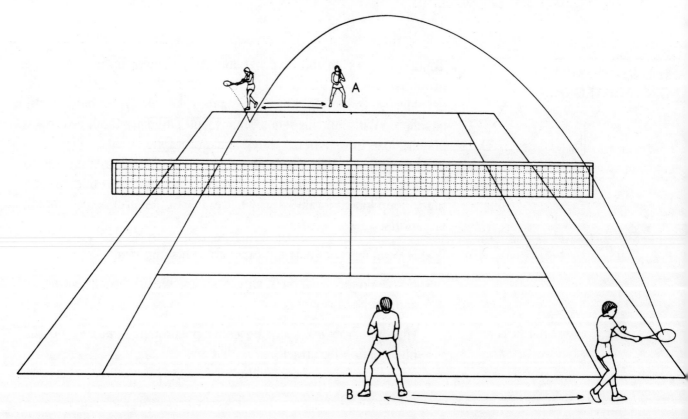

DRILL 11

Backhand Crosscourt Lob

The purpose and directions for this drill are the same as those for the forehand crosscourt lob drill.

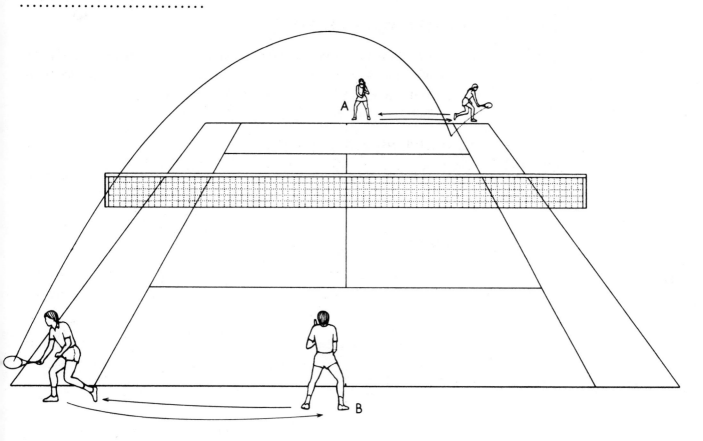

Forehand Down-the-Line
Lob
. . . .

The purpose of this drill is to develop deep and accurate down-the-line lobs by perfecting the elements of the Tennis Episode. As with down-the-line groundstrokes, down-the-line lobs require a target area six feet inside the baseline and well within the sidelines. Although difficult to produce, this shot often enables you to place an opponent in the position of having to hit a backhand overhead or some other hard defensive shot. The drill is the same for beginner and intermediate players; the advanced player follows the format of the forehand crosscourt lob drill.

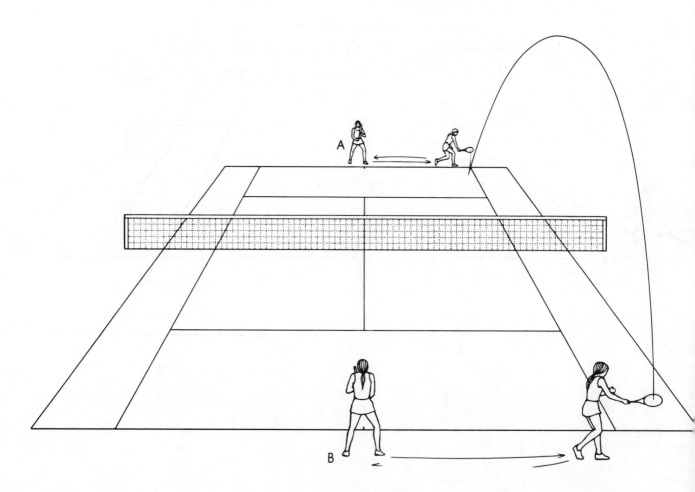

DRILL 13
_____

Backhand Down-the-Line
Lob
. . . .

The purpose and directions of this drill are identical to those for the forehand down-the-line lob drill.

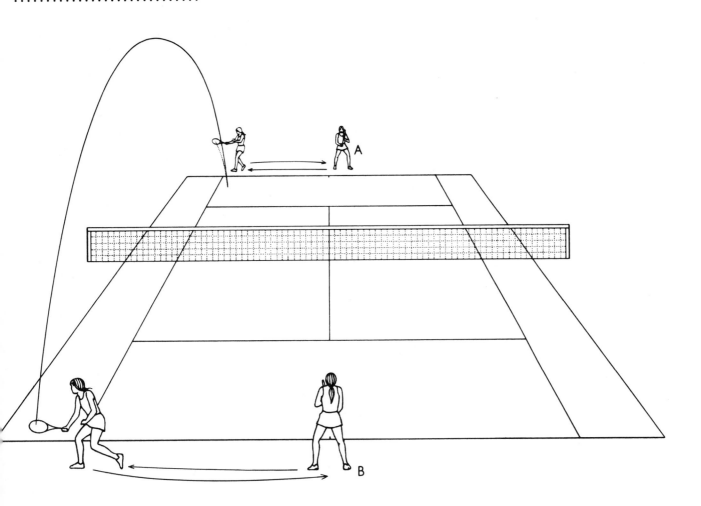

EXPLOSIVE MOVEMENT

Explosive movement is a vital attribute and goal of Tennis Kinetics. It means more than just being fast, it means being *quick*—quick enough to reach your top speed in two steps. That sort of quickness can only be realized through mental and physical preparation. Mentally you must attune yourself to one fraction of a moment that calls for an immediate and powerful response. Physically it means that you must train your body to respond correctly and automatically to this mental cue for action.

There are three elements within the Tennis Episode that call for explosive movement if you want to achieve high-caliber play: Reaction, Transition, and Recovery. Of the three, Recovery is most often overlooked. Many players react quickly to get to an opponent's ball, but few appreciate the necessity of explosive quickness *after* their own shots. In each of these three elements of the Tennis Episode, explosive training will give you more confidence in your movements. Against a tough opponent you may find yourself needing the added quickness just to get to every shot. By the same token, your own quickness will require explosiveness from your opponent, and many an opponent simply won't be able to achieve it, allowing you to take advantage of his errors before he can cover them up with court positioning. Moreover, explosiveness provides you with extra time to execute quality kinetic chains, opening up your options on the ball's height, speed, spin, and direction. With more time to execute your Tennis Episodes, you will be more efficient and save energy, and the momentum and power of one Episode will flow into the next.

For the reaction element, prime your body by putting it in the Ready Position with a well-timed split step. In the Recovery phase, your immediate and powerful response serves to start your body moving toward the proper court position. In such Repositioning you must often cover as much court as you did to get to the ball in the first place, so you will need as much explosiveness in the Recovery element as you did in the Reaction element. Think of the Recovery of your first shot as the beginning of your next. This puts time on your side immediately, and often proves the difference between taking advantage of an opponent or allowing him to take advantage of you.

A player who wants to make his movements more explosive can benefit greatly from the following drills. They are practiced by some of the world's best tennis players, and while you will not require any lofty credentials to perform them, you should certainly be in good health and physically fit, especially for the later drills. Look them over, and if there is any question in your mind that they may be too rough for you, consult your physician.

Before any of these drills, you should use the warm-up in the fitness section that follows. Your muscles must be prepared for explosive training; they should be warm and mildly stretched. Attempting to perform any of these drills with cold muscles—and practicing them (as you should) at the speed required during competition—could lead to an injury.

The following drills are necessary for training correct responses and making them explosive and automatic. The body movement they require develops ballistic functioning of the appropriate muscle groups.

DRILL 14

Hand-Clap Drill
······················

Two players face each other across and close to the net (see below). One holds a ball at shoulder height. The other holds his hands six inches apart. The first player drops the ball, and the second claps his hands as near to that exact moment as he can. Note how far the ball drops each time. By improving his focus on the ball, a player can improve his time in reacting to the ball drop. Repeat the drill five times.

DRILL 15

Mirror Drill

Players A and B face each other, with B in the Ready Position. Player A presses the ball against his racket, then sharply directs B to move in one of six directions: left, right, forward-left, forward-right, back-left, or back-right. Player B tries to react as soon as possible and simulates hitting a volley. As player B improves his reaction, player A should try to disguise his "shots." For example, he can turn the shoulder to the left and move the ball to the right; player B must focus on the ball very closely, or he will react to player A's shoulder instead of the ball.

DRILL 16

Cue Drill

Player B stands on the baseline facing Player A just across the net. Player A gives cues by holding the ball in front of him and moving it to one side, then the other. Player B works on turning the hips/shoulders quickly, taking three steps to one side and completing a full groundstroke, then coming back. Player A changes direction as soon as player B returns to the ready position.

DEVELOPING YOUR TENNIS KINETICS . . . .

128

Quick-Start Drill

Player A stands at the net with extra balls. Player B positions himself two feet behind the service line. Player A volleys soft shots to both sides of B. Player B returns the ball softly to player A. A moves B around the two service boxes. B works on focusing on the ball and quick starts. A keeps B moving by extending his shots to the side and hitting some behind B.

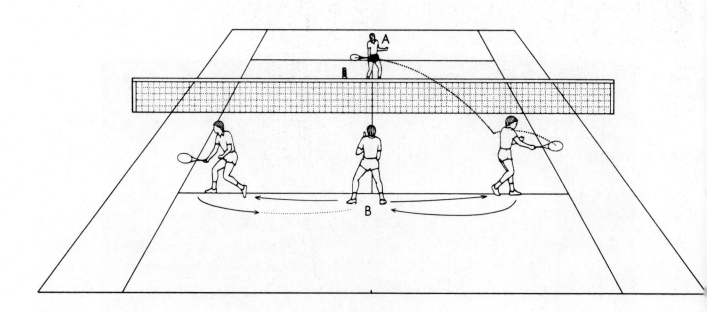

7 GROUNDSTROKE VARIATIONS

BEGINNER	1, 2, 4, 5
INTERMEDIATE	1–5
ADVANCED	1–5

Backstep

1 Rhythm Drill with Racket, No Ball
2 Rhythm Drill with Contact
3 Mixed Groundstrokes

One-Step

4 Rhythm Drill with Racket
5 Rhythm Drill with Contact

If You "Lose It" Drills

	GROUNDSTROKE VARIATIONS DRILL	CONNECTING	COMBINATIONS
Beginner	1, 2, 4, 5	1 A	1 A
Intermediate	2, 5, 3	2, 3	2 A
Advanced	2, 5, 3	2 and 3 or 4	2 A

THE REAPPEARANCE OF THE BACKSTEP
. . . .

In chapter 3 you learned the role of the backstep in the development of your overhead and how central the backstep movement is to the success of the smash. There are also times when a player needs to enlist the aid of the backstep while on the baseline.

A backstep variation of the groundstroke is useful when the ball has been directed right at your body or when it is coming high and deep into your baseline area. As always, you want to hit from the Strike Zone, and with this variation you need not assume some defensive, compromising position.

Almost any shot hit right at your body should be taken with the forehead groundstroke and the footwork of the backstep. Recall the moves for the overhead: As your hips and torso turn, you make a quick first step. If necessary, you follow with a cross-step, then normal running steps that take you well behind the bounce of the ball. From there you shift gears, moving forward toward the net. As the ball draws nearer to your Strike Zone, initiate the kinetic chain and make contact.

DRILL 1

Rhythm Drill with Racket, No Ball
. . . .

The purpose of this drill is to develop the backstep variation of the groundstroke.

Position yourself at the center of the baseline. Practice the footwork of the overhead, substituting the kinetic chain of the forehand groundstroke for that of the overhead. Then practice the footwork for the backhand smash, this time with the kinetic chain of the backhand groundstroke. Repeat, alternating forehand and backhand sides. (See footwork in photo sequences on pages 76–79.)

DRILL 2

Rhythm Drill with Contact
. . . .

The purpose of this drill is to coordinate the rhythm of the backstep groundstrokes with contact in the Strike Zone. It consists of duplicating groundstroke rhythm drills but with the following changes:

1. Player A feeds the balls directly at Player B.

2. The feeds are high and deep and are hit randomly to both sides of the court.

It is important that this drill be done correctly, or the players involved will develop bad habits. The feeder should make certain to allow Player B time to recover back to his starting position. Player B should move backward quickly, no matter how slowly the ball appears to be moving. Explosive positioning is crucial to the effectiveness of this stroke. Strive to make contact in the Strike Zone on every shot.

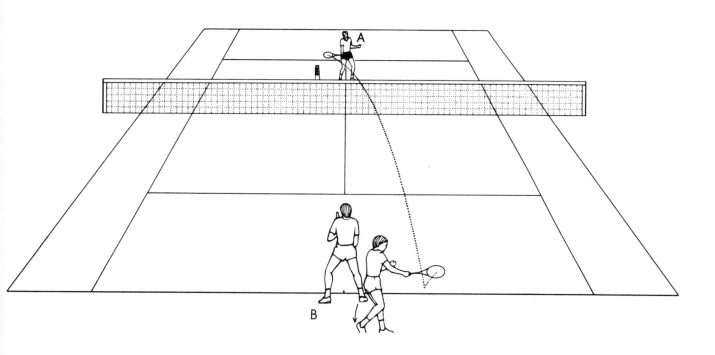

DRILL 3

Mixed Groundstrokes

The purpose of this drill is to read the ball quickly; to determine its direction, height, spin, and speed in order to respond with the correct footwork and groundstroke.

Repeat Drill 2, but with the feeder mixing the height and direction of his feeds—from average shots to shots hit high and deep; from forehand to backhand to shots hit directly at Player B.

THE ONE-STEP

Many shots come in only one step away from you, especially returns of serve and soft, high volleys, and also some groundstrokes. On returning such shots, use the one-step variation. It is a full-blooded groundstroke from the hips up, but footwork is limited to just one step.

DRILL 4

Rhythm Drill with Racket

The purpose of this drill is to develop the rhythm of the one-step.

In front of a full-length mirror, assume the Ready Position. Then, with full preparation of body and racket:

1. Turn the hips, torso, and shoulders; the racket goes back.

2. For a count of two, remain balanced in this position.

3. Step forward with the lead foot and initiate the proper kinetic chain.

4. Recover and reposition.

Practice this movement for both forehands and backhands.

DRILL 5

Rhythm Drill with Contact
....

This drill integrates your one-step with other groundstroke and backstep drills by having the feeder hit balls within one step of your starting position.

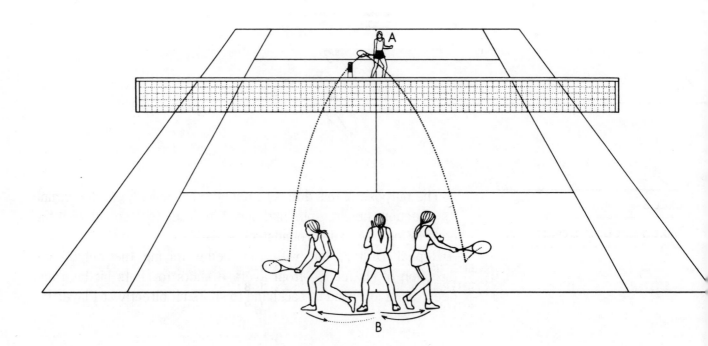

8 THE SERVE*

If You "Lose It" Drills

	SERVE DRILLS	CONNECTING	COMBINATIONS	
Beginner	3, 4, 6	1 C	9 A	
Intermediate	3, 6, 7	1 C	9 A or B, 10 A or B	
Advanced	4, 6, 8	1 C	10 A or B, 11 (12 and 14, Serve-and-Volley Players)	

*The grip for the serve is the Continental. (See page 106.)

DRILL 1

Kinetic Chain with Mirror

This drill is designed to encourage the smooth transfer of power from legs to hips to trunk to shoulders to arm, wrist, and ball.

Review the photo sequence on pages 94–95 and duplicate it in front of a mirror.

1. Start in the position shown in photo 3; both arms are together in the air.

2. In photo 4, the racket head drops behind the body as the hips rotate forward.

3. In photo 5, the racket moves up toward contact.

Observe your form in the mirror to make your motions match those of Martina. Repeat the sequence, gradually quickening the rotations of the hips and shoulders, and follow that chain of motion with the upward motion of the arm. Do not lead with the arm itself! Power starts from the lower body.

DRILL 2

Kinetic Chain with Racket

This drill is the same as drill 1, only you use a racket and focus your attention on the feeling of propelling the racket upward.

DRILL 3

Rhythm Drill with Mirror

The purpose of this drill is to develop the complete rhythm of the service motion.

Review the photos on pages 94–95. In front of a mirror, place yourself in the Ready Position, as in the first photo. Then duplicate the rhythm of the serve in the photo sequence:

1. Hands go down together.

2. Hands go up together.

3. Racket head drops behind as the hips rotate forward.

4. Racket moves to contact the ball, completing the cadence of "down-up—and hit."

Repeat this drill with your eyes closed and try to feel the complete rhythm of the serve's kinetic chain.

DRILL 4

Rhythm Drill with Racket

The purpose of this drill is to develop the service rhythm with racket in hand. A repetition of drill 3, it can be a good warm-up for your serve prior to a match and should be used whenever you feel the need to fine-tune your service rhythm.

DRILL 5

Kinetic Chain with Contact
. . . .

The purpose of this drill is to develop consistency in the coordination of toss and kinetic chain.

Refer to the photos on pages 94–95. Begin the sequence with ball in hand, resting on the thigh of your front leg, then lift the tossing arm to the position shown in photo 3. Toss the ball. Follow with the rest of the kinetic chain shown in photos 4 and 5.

Repeat the service motion until the toss is consistently and smoothly joined with the kinetic chain. Never lunge after a bad toss. Instead, begin again, adjusting the toss to fit the motion of the serve.

DRILL 6

Rhythm Drill with Contact
. . . .

The purpose of this drill is to develop the combination of rhythm, toss, and contact.

Review the entire photo sequence for the serve (pages 94–95) and duplicate the rhythm with a cadence of "1-2—3-4" (pause between 2 and 3) or "down-up—and hit."

Consistency of toss is the key to a rhythmical serve. A ball tossed too high will delay the rhythm: "1-2——3-4." A ball tossed too low will rush the rhythm: "1-234." You should make contact at the peak of the ball's toss.

In this drill, do not be overly concerned with the ball's direction upon contact; instead concentrate on the feel of the rhythm of the serve with contact.

DEPTH AND THE SERVE
. . . .

In serving as in hitting from the baseline, a player can fall prey to the illusion of depth. The serve ends up lower and shorter in the box than was intended or expected. For the beginner, simply finding the service box with some consistency may be good enough, but then it is time to become a more effective server. What makes a serve effective? The answer, of course, is depth.

DRILL 7

Depth in Serving
. . . .

The purpose of this drill is to develop height and depth in the serve.

Place a row of tennis balls across the service boxes as shown in the diagram below. The distance from the row of balls to the service line—your target area—should be two feet. Serve ten balls into the deuce box, then switch to the ad box.

With each practice session you should try to increase your percentage of shots into the target area by 10 percent, until you can serve at 70 percent or better. Once you have accomplished this, narrow the target area to one foot and repeat the process.

Use a rhythmic motion that produces moderate pace, and be certain to launch the ball upward off your racket. In this drill you are trying to achieve depth, so it is far better to err by hitting long on your serves than by hitting too short.

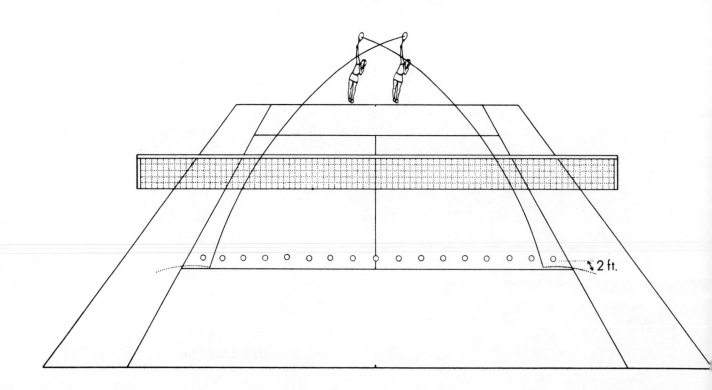

. . . . **THE SERVE**

137

DRILL 8

Serving with Depth and Direction
. . . .

This drill stresses direction along with depth in one's serving practice. It takes drill 7 a step further with two distinct target areas in each service box. Confine your first two serves in each box to the area bounded by the sidelines. After these four serves, aim for the interior areas bounded by the center line.

With the combination of concentrated height and direction you can improve your accuracy tenfold. If you can achieve a 70 percent accuracy rate in this drill, you have developed an extremely effective service.

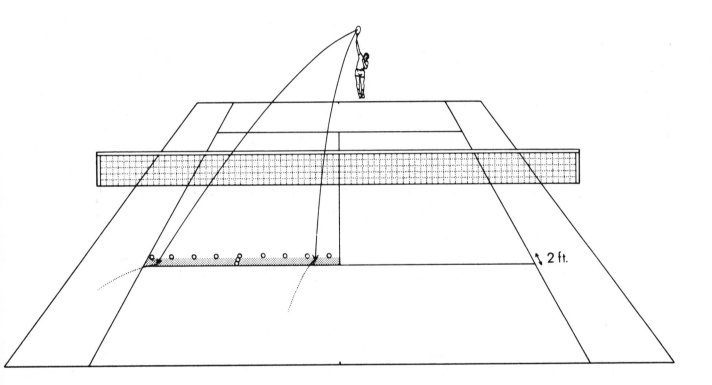

2 ft.

THE WEAK LINK IN SERVING

There is a well-worn, time-honored saying among tennis players: "You're only as good as your second serve." Of all the potentially weak links in a player's game, this has got to be the weakest of all. For this reason, a player should develop his second serve first—that is, a serve that will land deep under the pressure of a second-serve situation. By relieving the anxiety of producing well under such circumstances, the player will also find a marked improvement in his first serve. No longer riddled with self-doubt, his first serves will assume more strength and conviction, and thus diminish the need for a second ball.

Intermediate and advanced players must develop both spin and direction in their second delivery. More often than not the direction of choice is the receiver's backhand, though that might not always be an opponent's least favorite reply. Experiment when serving, moving the ball to both sides, also directly at the receiver's body. As for spin on the second serve, the advantages are many, but most importantly:

- Spin increases the margin of safety by driving the ball higher over the net and, at the same time, causing it to drop into the service box.

- Spin will change the behavior of the ball as it bounces, making it a difficult task for the receiver to judge where and when the ball must be intercepted. A spin serve is more difficult to return with authority than a flat serve.

THE POWER SERVE

In developing a powerful first serve the player must realize two things:

- Power is not as important to a server as accuracy. A combination of depth, spin, and angle is more devastating than speed alone (witness Martina Navratilova and John McEnroe).

- Power is first generated by the lower body, especially the legs and hips. Power does not come from one's wrist. To prove this, try to hold your forearm in place, ball in hand, while snapping your wrist and releasing the ball. Not much pace, right? The wrist serves only to transfer the power that builds in a player's body. Therefore, the way to improve the power of your serve is to quicken the rotation of hips and shoulders during the service rhythm.

. . . . **THE SERVE**

139

DRILL 9

Power Serving
. . . .

The purpose of this drill is to develop facility in hitting with both power and angle on the first serve.

Set up the court with the target areas shown in the diagram below. Starting with the deuce box, serve ten hard balls into the one-foot target area. Follow with ten spin serves into the same box, aiming into the five-foot area. Switch to the ad side and repeat.

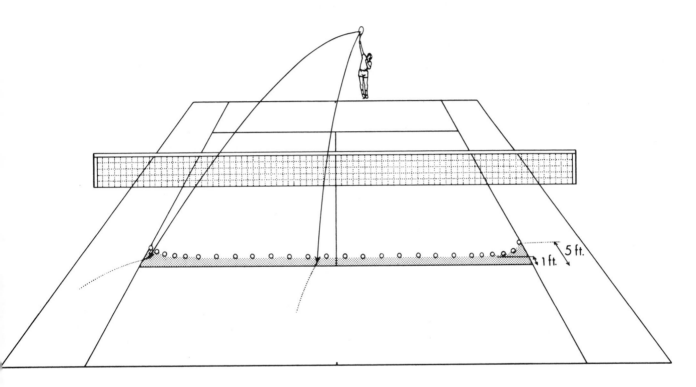

9 THE RETURN OF SERVE

BEGINNER	**1–3**
INTERMEDIATE	**1–3**
ADVANCED	**1–3**

1 Rhythm Drill with Racket, No Ball   **3** Ball Control
2 Rhythm Drill with Contact

If You "Lose It" Drills

	RETURN-OF-SERVE DRILLS	CONNECTING	COMBINATIONS
Beginner	1–3	1 A	9 A and B
Intermediate	1–3	3 B	9 A or B, 10 A or B
Advanced	1–3	3 B	10 A or B, 11, 14

To help you appreciate the complexity of the return of serve—a stroke that many players, even coaches, take for granted—know that a return of serve can involve the rhythms of groundstrokes (including all the variations), volleys, and approach shots. Beginners should use the rhythms of the groundstrokes only, but if you are an intermediate or advanced player, you must have the fluency of all three rhythms for consistently successful returns of serve. If you have not yet developed all of these rhythms, you should do so now, before proceeding.

The drills that follow are designed to develop the ability of a player to correctly respond to any serve with the appropriate rhythm.

- For serves hit hard and deep into the service box, use the volley rhythm.

- For serves hit softly and short into the service box, use the approach shot rhythm.

- For serves hit with moderate depth and speed, use a groundstroke (or variation of a groundstroke) rhythm.

- No matter what the serve, recover and reposition toward the center of the court. The grip is the same as that used for the groundstrokes.

DRILL 1

Rhythm Drill with Racket, No Ball
. . . .

The purpose of this drill is twofold: to develop the proper Ready Position, both body preparation and court positioning, for returning serve; and to develop all the return of serve rhythms with proper Recovery and Repositioning.

Refer to the following starting position diagrams and note the Ready (Court) Position. Practice each of the following rhythms, remembering to move *forward* into a good Ready Position before executing the appropriate rhythm:

1. Groundstrokes: forehands and backhands

2. One-step variation: forehands and backhands

3. Backstep: forehands and backhands

4. Lunge volley: forehands and backhands

5. Approach shot: forehands and backhands

Always complete each rhythm with accurate Recovery and Repositioning.

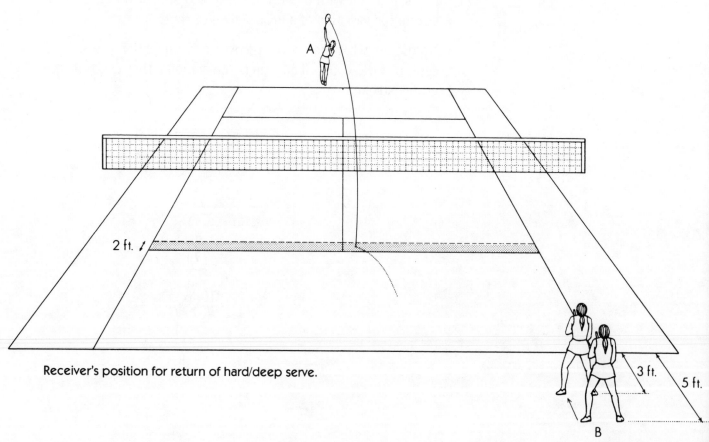

2 ft.

Receiver's position for return of hard/deep serve.

3 ft.

5 ft.

A

B

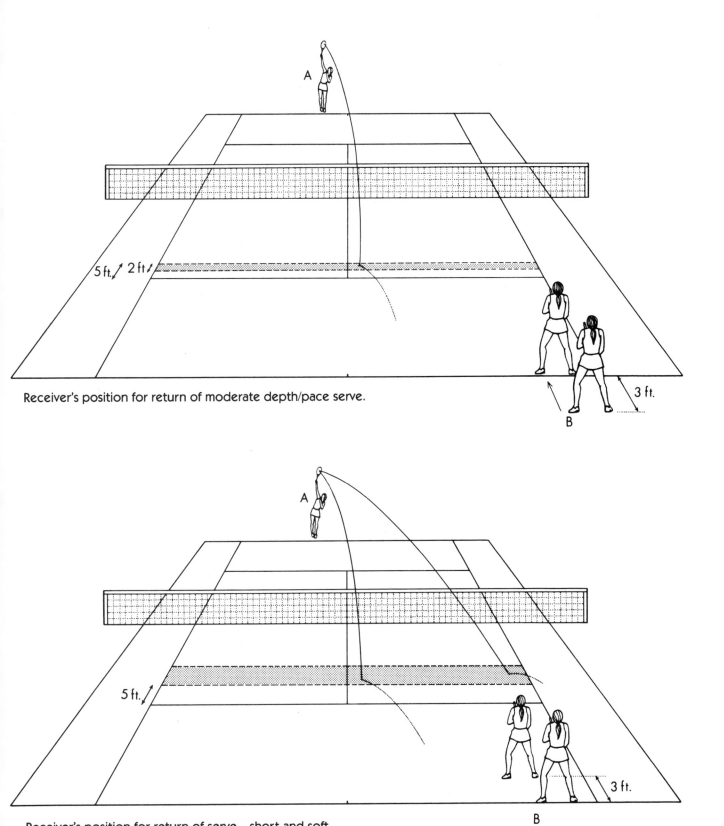

Receiver's position for return of moderate depth/pace serve.

Receiver's position for return of serve—short and soft.

DRILL 2

Rhythm Drill with Contact
· ·

DRILL 3

Ball Control
· ·

With a partner serving, practice the appropriate rhythms while locating each shot in your Strike Zone.

Intermediates and advanced players should ask their partners for a set of short serves to allow practice of approach shots.

The purpose of this drill is to develop control of height, direction, and pace for returns of serve.

Refer to the diagrams for targets. Beginners target their returns high and deep in the center (diagram 1). Intermediates and advanced players target as follows:

- Versus serve-and-volley players: low up the center, aimed to land on the service line (diagram 2).

- Versus groundstrokers staying at the baseline: deep, down the center (diagram 2).

- Versus short serves, especially on second serves: down the line, deep or crosscourt, low and angled (diagrams 3 and 4).

1. Return of serve—beginner target.

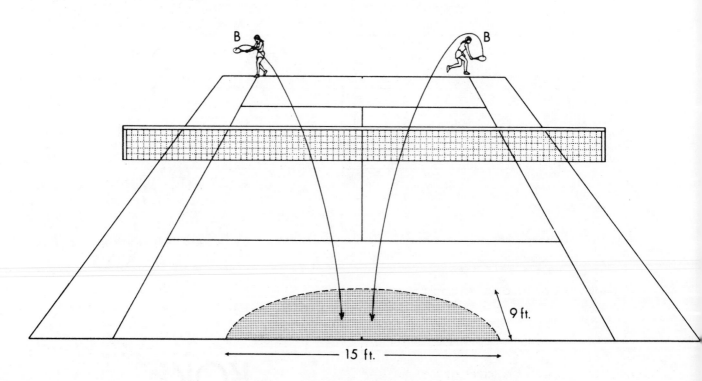

9 ft.

15 ft.

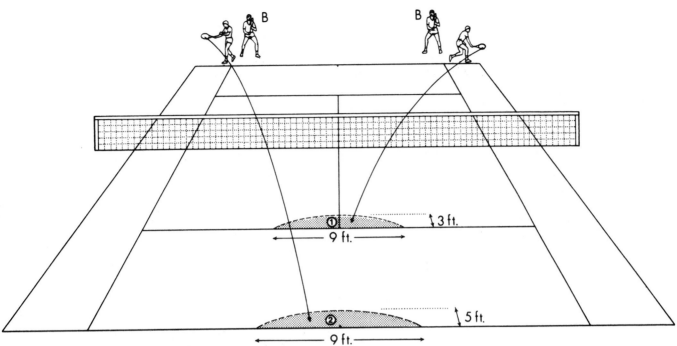

2. Intermediate and advanced targets: (1) versus serve-and-volley player, (2) versus baseliner.

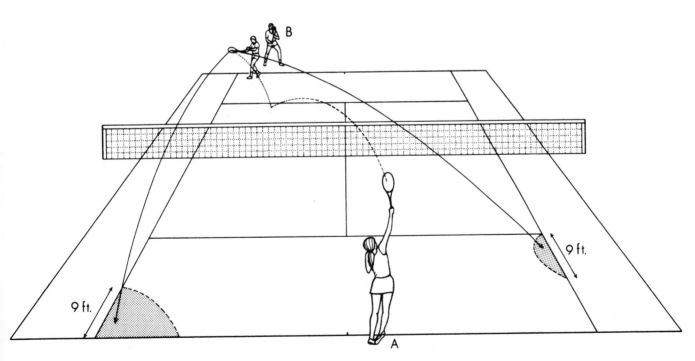

3. Return of serve versus short serves, deuce court.

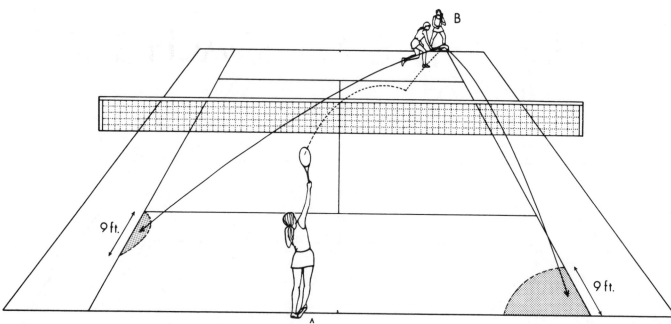

4. Return of serve versus short serves, ad court.

Intermediate and advanced doubles players should have a crosscourt, sharply angled target, keeping the ball low over the net and aimed to land at the junction of the service and singles sidelines (diagram 5). If you are an advanced singles player, once you can hit the basic targets described above, develop the ability to hit down the line and deep, also crosscourt and sharply angled.

Attain an 80 percent accuracy rate for the basics before developing these alternates.

5. Return-of-serve targets for doubles play.

10 THE APPROACH SHOT*

BEGINNER	**1–3**
INTERMEDIATE	**1–4**
ADVANCED	**1–4**

1 Rhythm Drill
2 Rhythm Drill with Contact

3 Ball Control with Feeder
4 Ball Control with Partner

If You "Lose It" Drills

	APPROACH SHOT DRILLS	CONNECTING	COMBINATIONS
Beginner	1, 2, 3	1 B	3
Intermediate	1, 2, 3	1 B	3 or 4
Advanced	4	1 B	4, 5 A and B

*The grip for the approach shot is the same as that used for the groundstrokes.

DRILL 1

Rhythm Drill
....

The purpose of this drill is to develop the strokes that allow for the smoothest transition from backcourt to forecourt. The drill places the focus on continuous forward movement and a shortened backswing.

Refer to the photo series below. Starting from the Ready Position, move directly toward the net, duplicating the turn, stroke, and Recovery of the photo sequence.

For the forehand approach: Your stroke should be timed so that you make contact between steps. For example, a right-handed player will go from right foot to contact and continue running. Avoid the error of making contact while on the front foot, which reduces the option of hitting crosscourt; it also usually requires you to stop, thus slowing down your approach to the net and often causing you to contact the ball late.

Rhythm drill for the approach shot.

1

2

For the backhand approach: Contact is made with the body in a moderately closed position, and may occur off either foot. The arm bearing the racket is in front of your body when you close your stance on the backhand, and thus you are not required to stop to contact the ball. You also do not sacrifice your crosscourt option.

Alternate from forehand to backhand approach shots, and punctuate each rhythm with a split step, as shown in the photo on page 74. Repeat this exercise until the running is smooth and continuous. At that point, accelerate your first step forward directly upon contact. In both these movements the approach shot must be explosive.

3

4

DRILL 2

Rhythm Drill with Contact
··

The purpose of this drill is to syncopate the rhythm and footwork of the approach shot with the moment of contact.

Situate yourself behind the baseline with ball in hand. Begin your forehand approach rhythm and toss the ball slightly in front of you. Using continuous movement and a shortened backswing, make contact with the ball between steps and well in front of your body. Once the ball has been struck, recover and continue to move forward until you are positioned at the net. Practice the backhand approach shot in the same manner. For both backhand and forehand shots, aim your approaches down the lines.

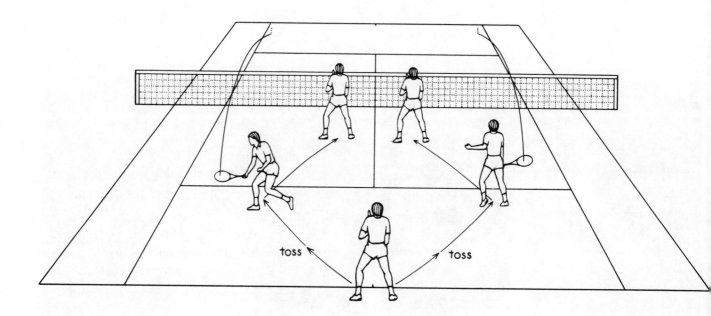

DRILL 3

Ball Control with Feeder
··

The purpose of this drill is to combine good approach shot rhythms with ball control.

Player A feeds a series of short balls (balls that bounce before the service line) to player B. The pattern should be deliberate at first, then random to both forehand and backhand.

Beginners should aim all of their shots down the lines. Intermediate and advanced players have three targets, as shown: down the line, deep up the middle, and low-angled, crosscourt.

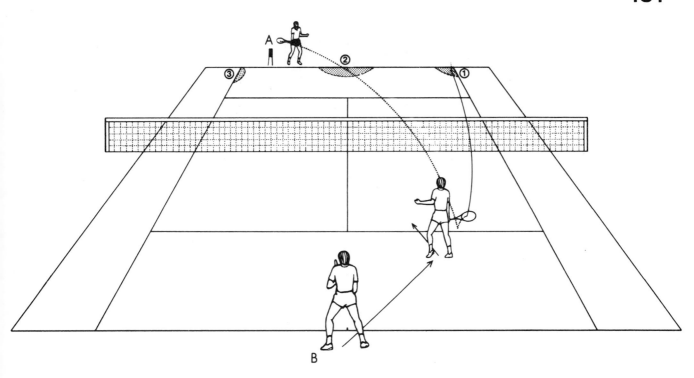

DRILL 4

Ball Control with Partner
·································

The purpose of this drill is threefold: to develop quick starts; to contact the ball before it drops below the height of the net; and to practice playing the ball on the rise.

Player A and Player B rally from the baseline. At some point Player A hits a short ball to player B, who approaches and aims for one of the targets used in drill 3. Simultaneously, Player B moves in to defend the net against a passing shot or lob. Upon completion, roles are switched.

THE WEAK LINK IN APPROACH SHOTS
·································

Players who suffer from weak approach shots tend to allow the oncoming ball to fall below the height of the net. By waiting too long before making contact, the approaching player must lift the ball upward instead of driving it into the opposite court. The net-rusher is then reduced to defending the net instead of attacking from his otherwise advantaged position, and very often he falls victim to passing shots and well-placed lobs.

Remember that a good approach shot begins with an explosive first step forward. Don't let the ball come to you—go after it just as quickly as you can.

11 THE VOLLEY

BEGINNER	**1–3**	
INTERMEDIATE	**1–3**	
ADVANCED	**1–4**	

1 Rhythm Drill with Mirror
2 Rhythm Drill with Contact

3 Ball Control
4 Explosiveness: The Goalie Drill

If You "Lose It" Drills

	VOLLEY DRILLS	CONNECTING	COMBINATIONS
Beginner	1, 2	3 A	3
Intermediate	1, 2	3 A	3, 4, 6, 7 A and B
Advanced	2, 3, 4	3 A, 4	4, 5 A and B, 7 A and B, 8

. . . . **THE VOLLEY**

153

The recommended grip for the volleys of most players is the same as that for groundstrokes—the Eastern grip. Many advanced players, however, having mastered the basic volley stroke, choose to use the Continental grip. This grip is used for serves, and can be used for all overheads and volleys, from either side. Especially for a net player, it can save time otherwise used to switch from forehand to backhand grips.

DRILL 1

Rhythm Drill with Mirror
. . . .

The purpose of this drill is to develop the proper rhythm for volleys. The drill stresses footwork and balance for maintaining the rhythms, with emphasis on the lower body movements.

These movements should be executed very slowly for improved balance. If balance is lost on the first step of the rhythm, begin again, holding that movement to the count of three, and proceed from there.

Study the photo sequences of forehand and backhand rhythms on pages 72–75. Duplicate the movements in a mirror, alternating from one rhythm to the other. Perform repetitions as well—two forehands, two backhands, etc.

DRILL 2

Rhythm Drill with Contact
. . . .

The purpose of this drill is to coordinate the rhythm of the volley with solid contact. Your goal is to time the rhythms so that you make contact just after your lead foot hits the court.

For the beginner: Player A is positioned just behind the service line, and feeds Player B shots with consistent pace and location.

For intermediates and advanced: Player A positions himself behind the baseline, first in one corner of the court, then the other, and alternates feeds to both forehand and backhand sides of Player B. Player A should alternate the sequences as well—two forehands, two backhands—and then feed randomly so that the direction of the balls cannot be anticipated by Player B.

Player A should take care to allow enough time between feeds for Player B to complete each rhythm and regain the Ready Position.

Player B should not target his shots. He is practicing rhythm only.

DRILL 3

Ball Control
....

The purpose of this drill is to develop the ability to direct volleys accurately. To do this requires that the player assume a good Ready Position before the ball is struck by his opponent, that he keep his racket head up, and that he be quick and smooth in completing his volley rhythms. Note the diagram below and the positions accordingly.

For the beginner: Beginners are given two targets—down the line (1) and crosscourt (2). Player A should direct both forehands and backhands to Player B, who aims first at target 1, then target 2. Player A can then feed sets of forehands and sets of backhands to Player B, alternating the targets with each set of feeds.

For intermediate and advanced players: There is an additional target, a sharp-angle shot (3).

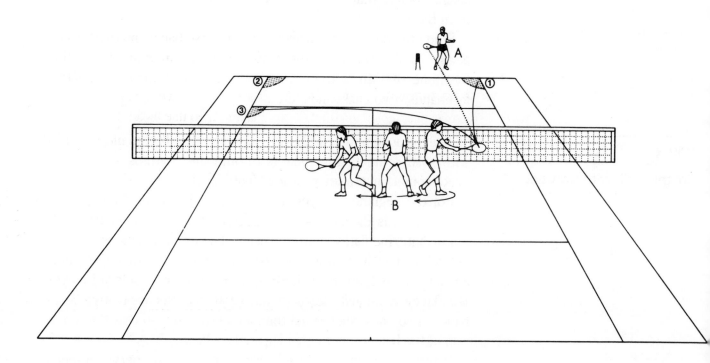

THE WEAK LINK IN VOLLEYS
· ·

There are three major weak links in the volley game.

Returning a low volley can present problems. A low volley is a defensive shot, so move in quickly and get to the ball before it drops below the net. If a low volley must be played, target your shot as close to the baseline as you can. Do not go for winners on low volleys!

Often a player will stand still and watch his volley during the time he should be Recovering and Repositioning for the next shot. This usually results in getting passed on the next shot. Make the Recovery step an automatic move. Reposition every time, unless you are sure you have hit a winner or have erred.

The high-backhand volley is particularly tricky. Practice this shot often, playing it deep down the line. An alternative is to angle the ball sharply, even though the percentages will be against you.

DRILL 4

Explosiveness: The Goalie Drill
· ·

The purpose of this drill is to develop explosive volley rhythms. The goal of the net player is to block every shot, and this requires concentration and keen reactions.

Refer to the diagram below and place two balls as shown, creating a "goal" for the feeder, Player A, to use as a target. Player B must prevent any ball from going into his "goal" by blocking it with volleys.

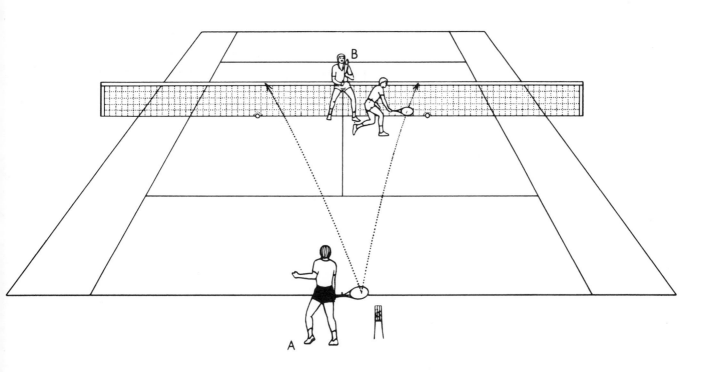

DEVELOPING YOUR TENNIS KINETICS . . . .

156

Player A gradually increases the speed of his feeds, though never without first allowing Player B sufficient recovery time between shots. The reason Player B positions on the same side of the net as Player A is to focus his attention on quickness and not concern himself with targeting his shots.

In the second phase of the drill, Player B moves to his proper side of the net. He now combines quickness of reaction and preparation with solid shotmaking.

12 THE OVERHEAD

If You "Lose It" Drills

	DRILLS	CONNECTING	COMBINATIONS
Beginner	1, 2	3 A	6
Intermediate	2, 3, 4	3 A	6, 7 A and B
Advanced	2, 4, 5	3 A, 4	7 A and B, 8

The key to a successful overhead is to get behind the lob—that is, to react so quickly as to reach a position from which you can move forward and produce a smashing kinetic chain. The grip for the overhead is the Continental, the same as for the serve.

DRILL 1

Rhythm Drill

The purpose of this drill is to develop the proper kinetic chain for the overhead. It is done with the racket but without the ball. Instead of striking the ball, then, you are stressing quick and early preparation of the hips, shoulders, and racket in coordination with smooth and balanced movement.

Refer to the photo sequence on pages 76–77. Starting slowly, duplicate the movements of the sequence, gradually increasing the speed of each motion:

1. Turn the hips and shoulders, while taking a step away from the net (photo 2).

2. Alternate your running steps away from the net.

3. STOP. Initiate your kinetic chain.

4. After simulating contact, move forward to where you started from and assume the Ready Position once more.

DRILL 2

Rhythm Drill with Contact Off a Bounce

The purpose of this drill is to incorporate the rhythm of the overhead with the proper point of contact. It requires the player to

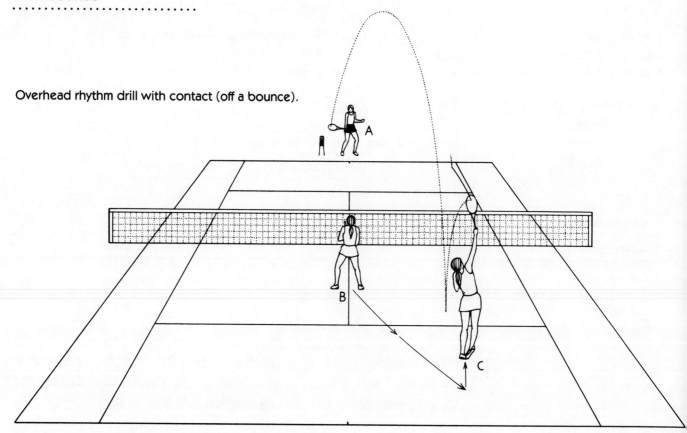

Overhead rhythm drill with contact (off a bounce).

move quickly to a position well behind the anticipated bounce of the lob, before connecting with the ball.

Refer to the diagram on opposite page and position yourself and your partner accordingly, with Player A at the baseline and Player B at net. Player A feeds high lobs, which should bounce between the service line and the net. Player B moves backward until he is comfortably behind the ball (c), then stops, moves forward, and contacts the ball. He may direct the ball anywhere on the court in this drill.

DRILL 3

Rhythm Drill for Forward Movement
. . . .

The purpose of this drill is to develop the skills necessary for smashing a lob before it bounces. Forward movement is most desirable for such a shot, so it is vitally important to prepare body and racket quickly and to maintain a clean stroke while moving toward the ball.

Position according to the diagram below: Player B is two steps behind the service line, Player A is behind the baseline. Player A feeds short, low lobs which, left alone, would land somewhere near the service line. Player B quickly moves forward, initiates his kinetic chain, and makes contact with the ball high and in front of his hitting shoulder. He may direct the ball anywhere in the court.

Overhead rhythm drill for forward movement.

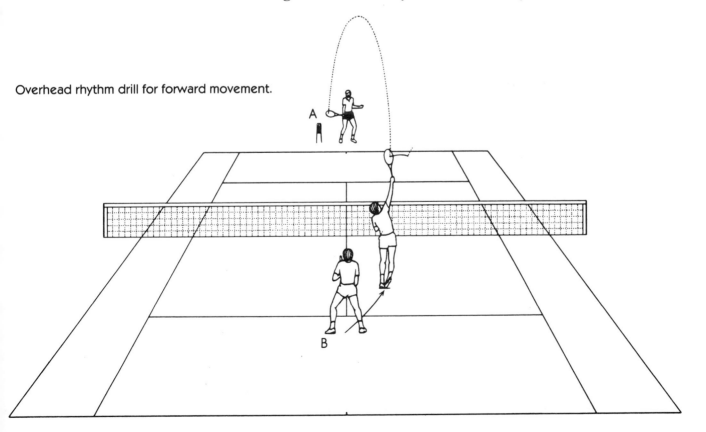

DEVELOPING YOUR TENNIS KINETICS ·

160

DRILL 4

Intercepting Lobs over Your Head

· ·

The purpose of this drill is to develop the overhead while moving backward for a lob. Quick and early movement is necessary here so that the player is able to get behind the arc of the lob.

Refer to the diagram below and position accordingly. Player A feeds Player B two types of lobs—high, short, and consistently placed; and deep and varied. With each feed Player B automatically runs back, adjusting his direction once he has fixed the depth and position of the lob. He then makes contact and assumes the Ready Position once again. He may direct his shots anywhere on the court.

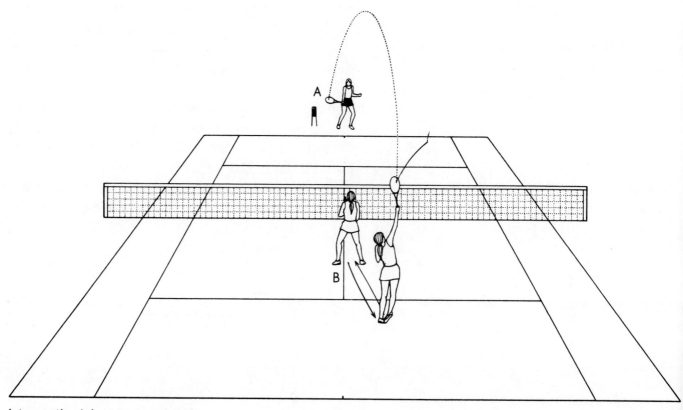

Intercepting lobs over your head.

DRILL 5

Ball Control Drill

The purpose of this drill is to direct overheads toward selected areas of the court, improving aim and depth perception.

Refer to the diagram below for position of players and targets. Beginners direct their overheads to target 1. Intermediates use targets 1 and 2. Advanced players aim for 2 and 3.

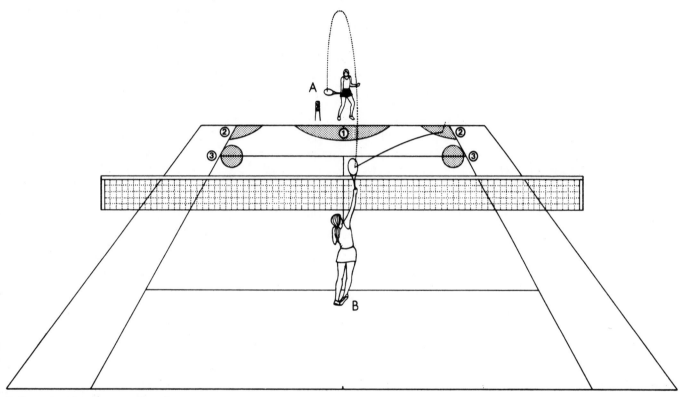

Ball control for the overhead.

THE WEAK LINK IN THE OVERHEAD

No matter how hard you try to hit your overheads on the forehand side, good opponents will find ways of getting the ball to your backhand. And no matter how good your backhand overhead gets, it will never equal the power of your forehand overhead. There is far less rotation of your body in the backhand position, with little chance for help from your shoulder, arm, and wrist.

When forced to hit backhand overheads, direct 80 percent to 90 percent of them down the line. By recovering and repositioning quickly, you will force your opponent to go for a winner if he is to claim the point. Go crosscourt only rarely—usually when you do, you will be a sitting duck for a down-the-line passing shot.

DRILL 6

The Backhand Overhead

The purpose of this drill is to develop a reliable backhand overhead. The important aspects of this shot are quick turns of the hips and shoulders, smooth running steps, and a concerted effort to keep the ball in front of your body.

Repeat drills 3 and 4, this time with lobs aimed to the backhand side. Your objective is to direct your replies deep down the line. As you progress, have the feeder alternate a few shots to your forehand overhead as well (advanced players should practice running around backhand overheads).

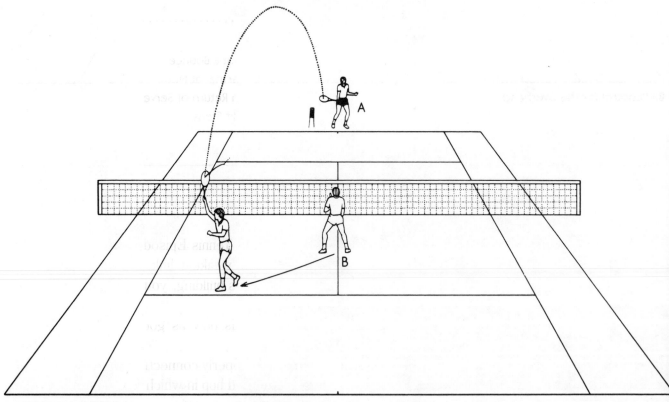

Backhand overhead.

13 CONNECTING TENNIS EPISODES: THE SPLIT STEP

In chapter 3 we introduced the Tennis Episode and explained why you are only as good as your weakest link. As your game progresses and you find your rallies building, you must take the weak link theory one step farther.

Your ability to play a point is only as good as your ability to connect good Episodes.

The technique we use for properly connecting Episodes is called the *Split Step,* a small two-footed hop in which the toes of both feet

DEVELOPING YOUR TENNIS KINETICS . . . .

164

point to the net. It is the one essential movement to poise yourself in line with your opponent's court. In fact, the split step should be integrated into all of the ball control drills of all the strokes, as well as all partner drills and serving drills.

The following drills have two purposes:

1. To develop the split-step technique so that you can transfer momentum smoothly from the end of one Tennis Episode to the start of the next.

2. To utilize the entire body properly in the split step—legs, hips, trunk, and shoulders.

As you practice these drills, remember always to get into a well-balanced Ready Position right after the ball bounces in your opponent's court, just before he makes contact.

DRILL 1

Timing the Split Step
. . . .

Review the appropriate diagram and practice groundstrokes, approach shots, and serves as follows:

a. *Groundstrokes:* Holding the ball in your forehand, assume a good Ready Position behind the baseline. Turn, run forward, toss the ball in front of you, hit (1), and recover. Watch the ball's flight as you reposition (2). Just after the ball bounces in the other court, perform the split step (3). The hop should bring you into a good Ready Position.

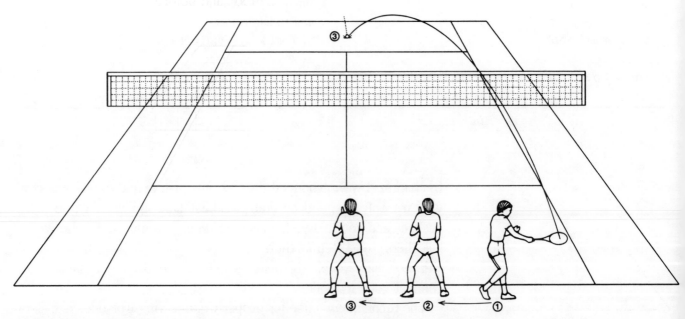

Connecting—timing the split step—groundstrokes: (1) hit, (2) recover/reposition, (3) when the ball lands (3) split step.

b. *Approach shot:* Perform this drill with the same technique as above, substituting the approach shot rhythm and repositioning for the groundstroke rhythm.

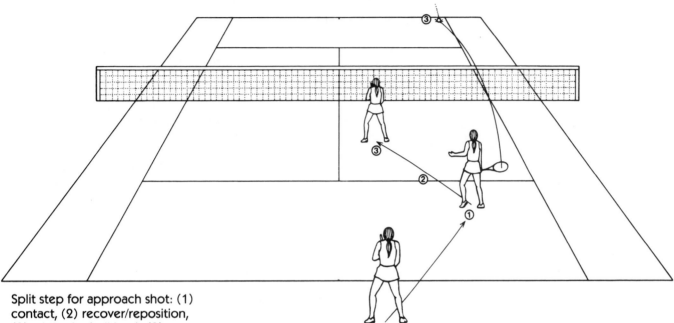

Split step for approach shot: (1) contact, (2) recover/reposition, (3) when the ball lands (3)— split step.

c. *Serve:* Serve the ball. Your Recovery step should regain your balance, and your repositioning should bring you back toward the baseline with the split step. You should make your split step just after the ball hits the service box and before your partner makes contact.

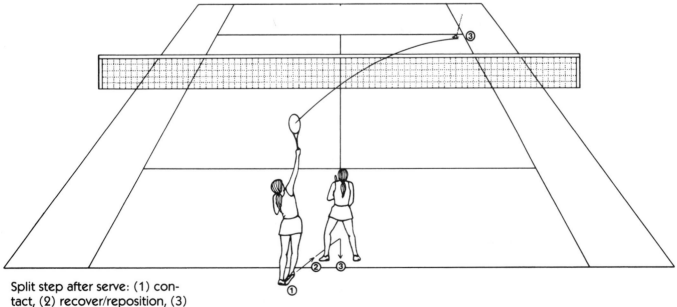

Split step after serve: (1) contact, (2) recover/reposition, (3) when the ball lands (3) split step.

DRILL 2
_____

Timing the Split Step for Connecting Episodes
. . . .

Review the diagram below. Rally with groundstrokes. Player A feeds Player B, who hits (1), recovers, repositions, and tries to time the split step correctly (2). (If player B's shot is high and soft, the split step will be delayed accordingly.) Player B's split step marks the start of his next Tennis Episode.

Perform only two Episodes at a time, until your timing is perfect. At that point, you can increase the string of Episodes and connecting split steps until you find yourself producing several high-quality connections in a row. Note that it helps to keep the balls high over the net to allow time enough for Recovery and Repositioning with split steps.

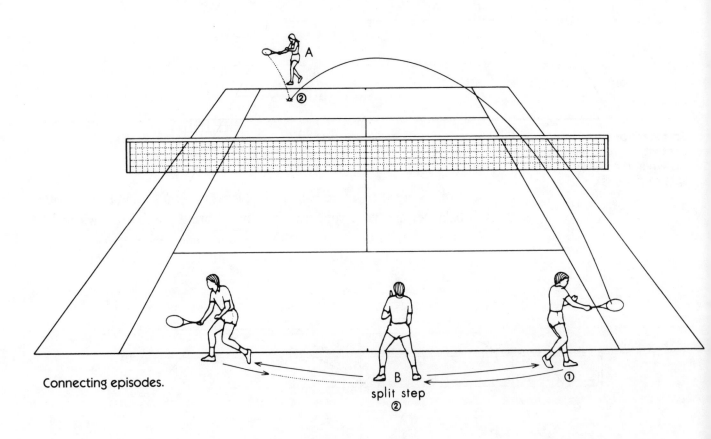

Connecting episodes.

. . . . **CONNECTING TENNIS EPISODES: THE SPLIT STEP**

167

DRILL 3
_____

Timing without a Bounce
. . . .

The purpose of this drill is to develop timing for the split step for balls that do not bounce before your opponent's contact: volleys, overheads, serves.

a. Repeat drill 2 with a partner at the net. Player A feeds to Player B, and Player B hits back to Player A at the net. There is no bounce, so Player B has to recover quickly and time the split step so that it occurs just before the ball reaches Player A's racket. (You may have to limit Repositioning depending on the time remaining for Recovery and split step.) Player A volleys to B. Player B

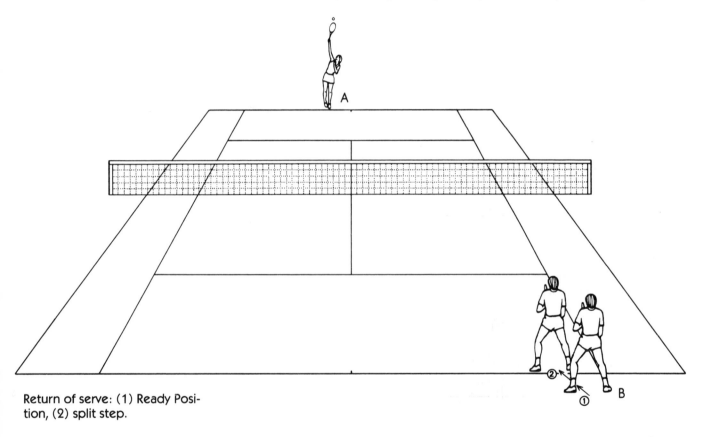

Return of serve: (1) Ready Position, (2) split step.

repeats, reacting from the split step into his Episode and ending each Episode with another split step.

b. For the return of serve: Player A serves to Player B, who is positioned behind the baseline. As Player A begins his toss, B moves forward and into his split step, which begins his reaction into his return-of-serve rhythm. This technique is used for overheads as well as serve, except that when returning an overhead player B does not move forward before his opponent contacts the ball.

DEVELOPING YOUR TENNIS KINETICS . . . .

168

Split step without the bounce
versus overheads—split step just
before contact.

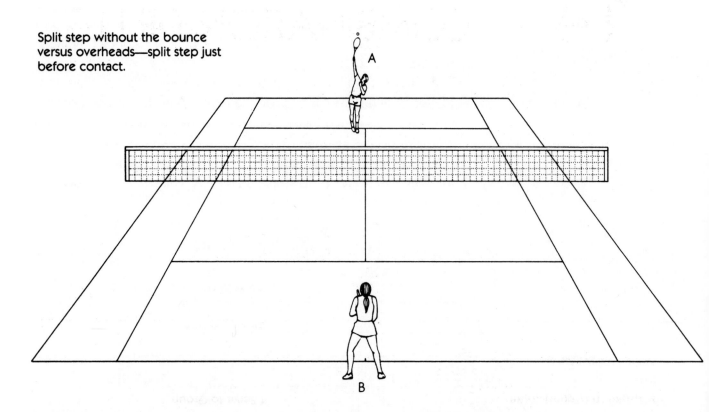

DRILL 4

For Advanced Players Only: Explosive Split Steps
. . . .

The purpose of this drill is to develop quickness in the timing of the split step.

Players A and B position themselves at opposite service lines and volley to one another, starting with high and slow-paced touch volleys, and stepping up the pace as improvement allows. Balls should be directed so that they are easy to control, since the split step occurs immediately after contact in this drill. Time and quickness are at a premium, with no time for the usual Recovery and Repositioning steps.

14 COMBINATION DRILLS

The drills in this section are designed to develop your ability to connect rhythms in various combinations:

- Groundstroke to groundstroke.

- Groundstroke to approach shot to volley.

- Volley to overhead.

- Serve to groundstroke.

- Serve to volley.

- Return of serve to groundstroke.

- Return of short serve (approach shot) to volley.

GROUNDSTROKE TO GROUNDSTROKE
. . . .

DRILL 1

Feeder
. . . .

a. Eight to Make Forty

Player A at net, B at baseline. Player A feeds shots requiring groundstrokes from B in the backcourt. B controls the ball with moderate pace back toward A. A follows with separate balls, moving B around the backcourt. B performs groundstrokes, or one of two variations: the backstep or one-step. The object is to hit forty balls with fewer than eight errors.

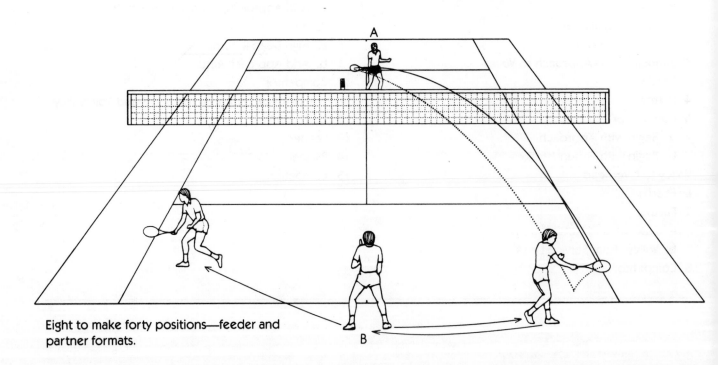

Eight to make forty positions—feeder and partner formats.

b. Two-by-Two Drill

There are two roles: feeder (A) and stroker (B). Each role develops accuracy and consistency. As stroker you develop quickness, court positioning, and ball control. Be sure to play each role every time you practice the drill.

Refer to the diagrams below and on the next page. Position as illustrated for round 1. Each round consists of four shots. The feeder begins in his forehand corner, which also serves as the target for the shots of the stroker. The feeder strokes two crosscourt shots, followed by two down-the-line shots, making sure they are well into the corners. The stroker returns all four shots, his target area being the corner where the feeder is positioned. After each shot, the stroker must concentrate on Recovering and Repositioning as he would for a shot that landed in that target area in a match.

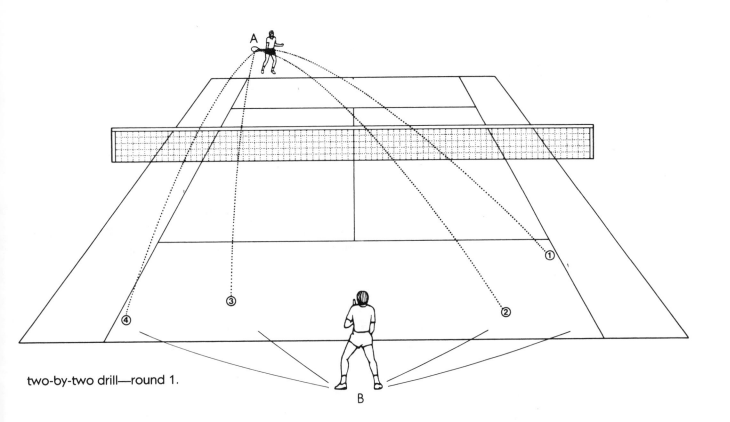

two-by-two drill—round 1.

For round 2, the feeder relocates to the other corner and feeds with his backhand in the same sequence. The stroker uses this new location as his new target for all four shots of the round.

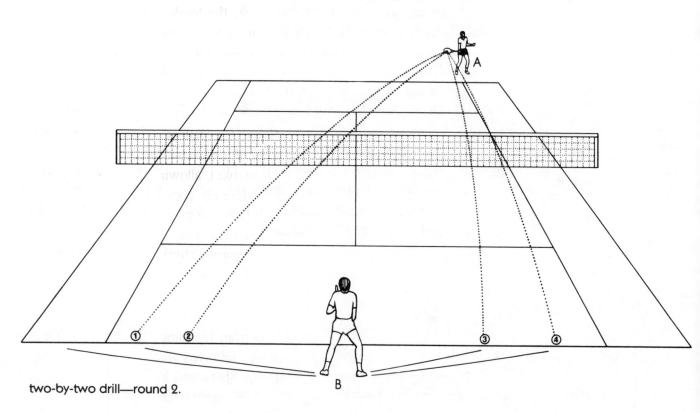

two-by-two drill—round 2.

DRILL 2

Partner
....

a. Eight to Make Forty

With B at the baseline and A at net, A feeds shots as in the previous eight-to-make-forty drill. In this drill, however, A volleys the responses back, requiring B to hit groundstrokes and variations. Play is continuous with B controlling the ball back to A. The objective: Forty shots with fewer than eight errors.

b. Two-by-Two Drill

Position and objectives are the same as for the previous two-by-two drill. The difference in this drill is that play is continuous—that is, A keeps B's shots in play, directing them in the proper sequence. There are two forms of the drill:

Version 1: Player B switches targets after four shots as in the feeder drill, stopping play while the feeder relocates.

Version 2: Player B switches targets without stopping after the fourth shot. Feeder A automatically shifts his position and continues to hit two consecutive shots to each corner.

. . . . **COMBINATION DRILLS**

173

GROUNDSTROKE—APPROACH—VOLLEY

DRILL 3

Feeder

A and B position at baseline. A, the feeder, introduces several balls as groundstrokes, then hits a short ball that B uses for an approach shot, continuing to the net. A feeds B a volley.

A should randomly mix sides for groundstrokes, approaches, and volleys.

DRILL 4

Partner

A and B position at baselines. One ball is played continuously between A and B. After trading groundstrokes, A hits a short-ball response (to B's second groundstroke), allowing B to approach and come to net, where A hits moderately paced low shots (two to three feet above the net) and B hits volleys.

The object for both is to keep the ball in play long and well enough to complete all of the separate rhythms: groundstrokes, approach shots, "passing shots" by A, and volleys by B.

DRILL 5

Competitor

a. Version 1:

Player A hits approach shot from his hand (forehand or backhand). B, positioned at baseline, receives the approach shot and plays out the point, with passing shots and lobs. A plays out the point following the approach shot with volleys and overheads. Switch roles every five points and keep score. Twenty-one points wins.

b. Version 2:

From the baselines, A and B trade groundstrokes and play out the point. A begins with groundstroke, which can be refused by B. After that first point the loser of the previous point starts the rally. Twenty-one points wins.

VOLLEY—OVERHEAD

DRILL 6

Feeder

A at baseline, B at net. A feeds one ball at a time using low and moderately paced shots or lobs, requiring forehand and backhand volleys and overheads from B.

DRILL 7

Partner

. . . .

a. Version 1:
Player A at baseline, B at net. B targets volleys and overheads back to A. A responds with low shots or lobs designed to keep the ball in play.

b. Version 2:
A and B are positioned at opposing service lines. Their objective is continuous play. A and B exchange volleys with moderate pace. The ball should travel two to three feet above the net. Mix sides, requiring both forehands and backhands.

DRILL 8

Competitor

. . . .

A and B are positioned on opposing service lines. A begins, and the players exchange three shots before trying to win the point. Loser of the last point starts the following point. Each time an error or winning point is made, score one point. Twenty-one points wins.

SERVE OR RETURN OF SERVE TO GROUNDSTROKE, APPROACH, ETC.
. . . .

DRILL 9

Feeder

. . . .

a. Version 1:
Deep serves (both first and second). A is the receiver, B the server. B serves deep into deuce court first, then ad court. For each serve, A returns a groundstroke high and deep down the center, or in either corner, requiring B to follow with groundstrokes or groundstroke variations.

b. Version 2:
Repeat drill above with the following additions: A should respond to serves that land well inside the service line with approach shots directed down the line. He should then follow the ball to the net, with B required to hit passing shots or lobs.

DRILL 10

Partner

. . . .

a. Version 1:
B serves deep first and second serves. A responds with return directed high and deep toward the center. A and B continue to keep the ball in play with groundstrokes, two shots each. Repeat, alternating ad and deuce courts.

. . . . COMBINATION DRILLS

175

b. Version 2:

As above with the following addition: short serves by B should be taken as approach shots by A and followed to the net. Play continues with B trying to pass A and A keeping the ball in play for B.

DRILL 11

Competitor
. . . .

Mark off a court as illustrated in the diagram below—that is, with one line four feet inside the service line and another nine feet inside the baseline (you can place balls in the alley to designate boundaries). Serves landing between the four-foot line and the service line are considered "deep" for this drill, and those landing between the net and the four-foot line are considered "short." Returns of serve landing between the nine-foot line and the baseline are "deep," while those landing between the nine-foot line and the net are considered "short."

A and B play out a point in which the server stays back after his serve (no serve-and-volley). Serves that land deep must be returned high and deep. Serves that land short require approach shot returns of serve, with the receiver advancing to the net. Varying from these requirements loses the point for the returner.

If an appropriate return is made, the point is played out. If, after five shots, neither player wins the point, each gets a point.

Competitor drill—serve/return of serve.

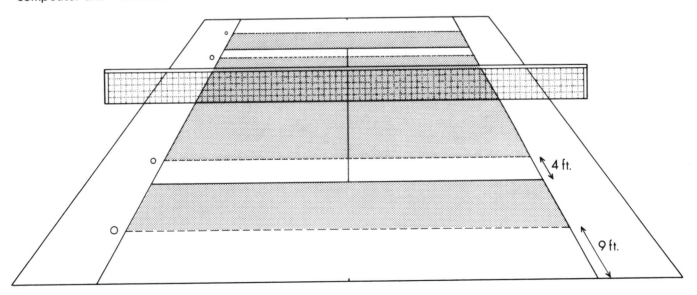

DEVELOPING YOUR TENNIS KINETICS . . . .

176

SERVE-AND-VOLLEY

. . . .

DRILL 12

Rhythm

. . . .

The purpose is to develop a good combination of rhythms for the serve-and-volley. Refer to the diagram below. The proper sequence of movements is:

1. Perform the service rhythm.

2. Move forward with three quick steps.

3. Split step.

4. Volley rhythm or approach shot.

5. Move forward to the appropriate net position.

Practice the sequence repeatedly, mixing forehand and backhand volley rhythms. Begin with slow, balanced movements to make sure of accuracy. As your performance improves, increase the speed of the above sequence of steps.

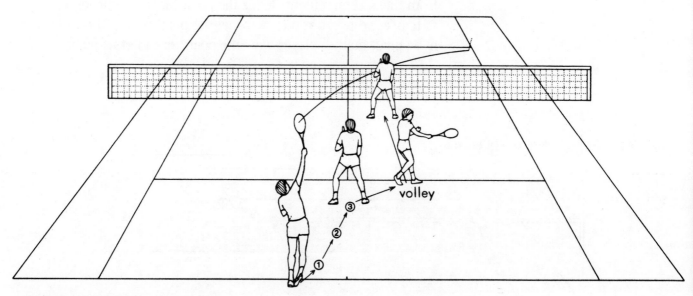

Rhythm drill for the serve-and-volley.

DRILL 13

Feeder

Refer to the diagram below. The purpose of this drill is to develop the serve-and-volley, with a feeder to hit returns that require volleys.

A positions as the player returning serve. Player B serves into the service box where A is positioned. B follows the serve with forward movement and the split step. A does not return B's serve, but replies with a shot requiring a volley from B, just after B makes the split step. B then volleys and moves forward to the appropriate net position, where A feeds another volley.

Repeat with A positioning in both the deuce and ad boxes, and mixing forehand and backhand volleys for B.

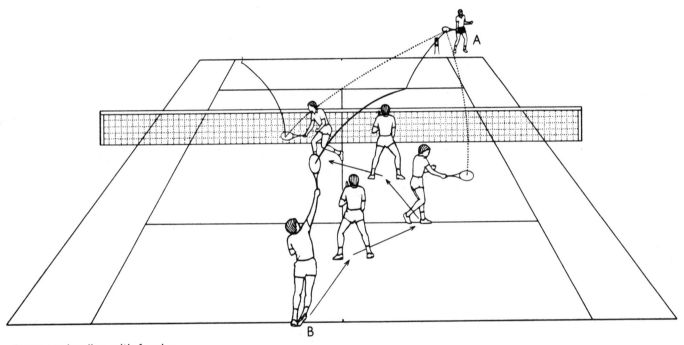

Serve-and-volley with feeder.

DRILL 14

Partner
. . . .

B serves and volleys as in the above drill. A now returns B's serve. A's return travels two to four feet above the net and to either the forehand or backhand side of B. A and B play for a total of three shots each and stop. A then mixes moderately paced low shots with lobs, while B responds with volleys and overheads designed to keep the ball in play for another three shots. Try to keep the ball in play; don't go for winners.

DRILL 15

Competitor
. . . .

Play out the serve-and-volley points. Only serve-and-volley may be used by the server. If A, the receiver, plays three shots without an error, or to the end of a point, he wins and scores one. Switch roles every ten points.

Return of Serve to Groundstroke, and **Return of Serve (approaches) to Volley and Overhead** are drilled by using the **Serve to Groundstroke** and the **Serve-and-Volley** combinations.

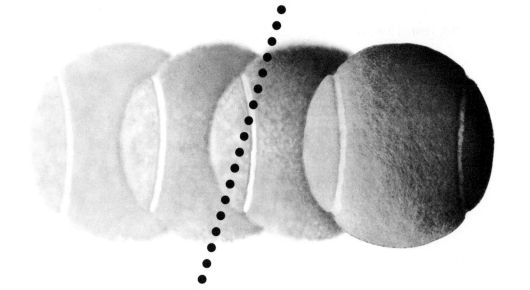

THREE

PHYSICAL FITNESS FOR TENNIS KINETICS

15 THE PROGRAM

To go with the developmental program we have just presented, we want to give you an equally full, incremental, and flexible program of fitness training that will help you get the most out of Tennis Kinetics. It is a year-round program designed to enhance and develop your game through the spectrum of kinetic proficiency, whether you are a beginner, an intermediate player, or of advanced caliber.

Certain physical abilities are necessary to the successful performance of Tennis Kinetics. Only by developing these abilities separately and then merging them can one achieve optimal performance. As with the kinetic chains for other sports discussed early in the book, each part of the whole is dependent upon the others, and if one ability is not at the level of the others, the entire performance is compromised.

What are the specific abilities that constitute the elements of fitness for the tennis player? There are six:

1. Flexibility

2. Strength

3. Power

4. Balance

5. Coordination

6. Quickness

The training program that follows offers a separate group of exercises for each of the first three elements—flexibility, strength, and power—with the other elements benefited under the third group. Throughout our presentation of these exercises, we will also discuss the importance of total fitness to the kinetic chains of tennis and show how the marriage of the two will bring optimal performance on the tennis court.

When it comes to actual practice, to the program itself, we do not expect you to perform these exercises one after the other . . . except for the first group—exercises for flexibility. These constitute the essential preparation—of warm-up and stretching—to any session of strength-and-power exercises. They should be considered a "curtain raiser" to each and every fitness training session, similar to the kinds of exercise that precede any type of aerobic or anaerobic training (and anaerobic endurance is very much a component of fitness for Tennis Kinetics). The stretching exercises are then to be repeated after every session of strength-and-power exercises.

How, then, are the strength-and-power exercises programmed and distributed in actual practice? Or to put it another way, one that relates them to the central premise of Tennis Kinetics, how are these separate elements merged into an effective chain, in this case a chain of physical fitness? It all comes together in the fourth and last chapter of this section, in a unique program of *cycle training* that combines the exercises for strength and power in tennis, at various levels of development, that are presented in the section's second and third chapters.

The initial reaction to the idea of year-round training, even for committed recreational athletes, is often one of dismay and turnoff, with thoughts of boredom, long workouts, and tedious attention to rigorous schedules. But it doesn't have to be that way, not if you vary your training with periods of what we call "active rest," according to a calendar approximated at the end of the cycle training chapter. With that final scheduling factor settled, you will be able to chart your own personal program of fitness training for Tennis Kinetics, joined with the developmental program of the preceding section.

These are, we believe, the best exercises you can practice for tennis proficiency. Through our program of cycle training, they offer, moreover, all the requirements for general fitness met by generic programs, and thus can supplant any such program you

. . . . **THE PROGRAM**

183

may be following now. A word of caution, however: Specific training programs such as ours are designed to achieve different goals than the generic programs with which you may be familiar. Even if you are currently in regular training, our program may work different muscles and energy systems from those involved in your present routine. Therefore we advise you to consult your general physician before you begin to participate in the training program that follows. Be sure to ask him whether he feels you should take any precautions, or perhaps omit certain exercises.

16 FLEXIBILITY

This component of performance is related to the elasticity of muscle tissue. Each joint of the body must allow for a certain amount of movement to and from the limbs, trunk, neck, and head in order for a person to accomplish even the most ordinary of daily activities. If joint movement, known as "range of motion," is limited, so too are the tasks performed by the joints. And a major consequence of limited joint motion is limited elasticity of muscle tissue. Players with "tight muscles" often give inhibited performances. They are also prone to such tennis-related problems as patella femoral pain, "frozen shoulder" syndrome, and lower back pain. Tennis demands many skills, skills that require flexibility in all joints of the body, and a lack of such total flexibility does more than hamper one's playing style; it increases greatly the chance of injury.

The following flexibility exercises build up one's range of motion. Tennis Kinetics insists on total body participation. A player who is flexible enough to perform all the necessary skills of Tennis Kinetics can perform at his most efficient level and with maximum enjoyment of the game.

WARMING UP

Proper training always requires a warm-up period, the purpose of which is to develop a progression of activity that raises the core temperature of the body and brings the system to an efficient state of readiness. David Balsley mentioned in chapter 2 that New York

. . . . FLEXIBILITY

185

City marathoners who had merely stretched before racing had 50 percent more injuries than runners who had warmed up properly as well—with easy jogging, calisthenics, or other simple activity. For tennis players too, a warm-up is an important prelude to stretching.

An effective warm-up can be achieved merely by jogging in place for three to five minutes. You will know when you have warmed up sufficiently when your core temperature is raised to the point where perspiration is imminent or has occurred. Your heart rate should be elevated but not racing. And don't be concerned about "looseness." This is purely a subjective concept. Athletes may or may not feel "loose" when they've completed their warm-up, but they should feel prepared to progress their activity to a more stressful level.

HOW TO STRETCH

A good stretching period comes next, under the following guidelines:

1. Stretch to the point of *mild* discomfort and hold for the recommended period of time.

2. Do not bounce the body part being stretched.

3. Progress slowly. It takes time to become flexible.

4. Stretch both before and after completion of the exercise period.

5. Stretch every day (even days when you are not performing a cycle training session).

All of the following exercises should be performed both before and after the exercises in your cycle training sessions. This segment of your training should take no more than twenty minutes a day.

STRETCHING EXERCISES

1. Low leg stretch (for calf muscles). Stand eighteen to twenty-four inches from a wall. Place the palms of both hands against the wall, keeping the heels of both feet flat on the ground and the back straight. Lean forward until your chest touches the wall. Hold this position for ten seconds and repeat two or three times. As you progress, stand farther from the wall.

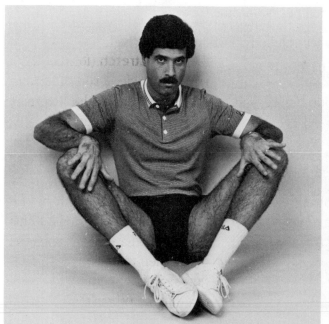

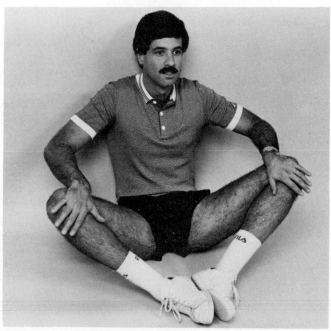

2. Inner thigh stretch (for the adductor muscle group). Sit on the floor with knees apart and the soles of your feet together. Place your hands on the insides of your knees and press downward, trying to get the outside of your legs as close as possible to the ground. Hold this pose for ten seconds. Repeat two or three times.

3. Hip stretch (for the abductor muscle group). Place either hip two feet from a wall. Place your hand against the wall and lean your hip toward it until a stretch is felt. Hold for ten seconds, return to starting position, and repeat two or three times. Repeat the exercise with the opposite hip. Progress by standing farther from the wall.

4. Quad stretch (for the quadricep muscle group). Stand erect, with the left hand against a wall to maintain balance. Keeping the left knee pointed straight down, raise and hold the left ankle with your right hand. Pull straight up in an attempt to have the heel touch the buttock. Hold for ten seconds, then repeat two or three times. Follow with same exercise for the other leg.

5. Hamstring stretch (for hamstring muscle group). Lie on your back and extend one leg upward at a ninety-degree angle (perpendicular to the ground). Kick the leg up slowly but strongly, without jerking, until it is straight up (or as high as possible). Hold for ten seconds and repeat two or three times, then alternate legs. Progress by bringing the knee toward the chest before straightening the leg.

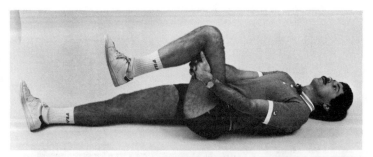

6. Low back stretch (for lower back muscle group). Lie on your back on a hard surface with knees bent. Place both hands around the left knee and pull toward your chest. Hold for ten seconds, then relax—first the leg, then the lower back. Repeat two or three times, then switch to the right knee.

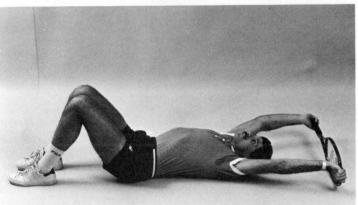

7. Shoulder girdle stretch. Lying on your back, hold a tennis racket as shown, with hands approximately shoulder width apart. Keeping your elbows straight, raise the racket over your head and backward until both arms are against the ground, or until you feel the stretch. Hold for ten seconds and repeat two or three times. Progress until the arms touch the ground.

8. Shoulder rotator cuff stretch. In a standing position, hold one end of a towel in your right hand, behind your back. Move your left hand to the small of your back and take hold of the other end of the towel. "Dry off" your back by pulling slowly up and down, going as far as you can and holding each pull for ten seconds. Repeat two or three times, then change hand positions. Progress by shortening the distance between hands.

9. Wrist stretch (for the wrist flexors). Make a flat surface of your right hand and place the fingers against the palm of your left. Push the fingers back until a stretch is felt. Hold for ten seconds, then repeat two or three times. Change hands.

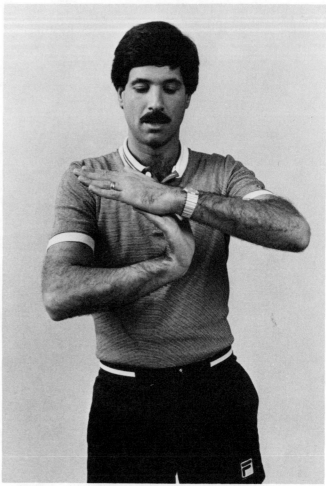

17 STRENGTH

Strength is the amount of force that is exerted by a muscle. An athlete can never be too strong so long as he has not compromised other components of fitness for the sake of strength alone.

In chapter 2 David Balsley spoke of the need for various muscles of the body to control and stabilize the joints so that an athlete can move in any direction, at any speed. An increase in the strength of one's muscle stabilizers results in a better performance. A tennis example: When serving, you must transfer the forces of the legs and hips to the upper body by utilizing your abdominal strength; if this muscle group is weak, your ability to transfer the forces from the lower extremities to the upper body will be weak as well.

There are other reasons to build body strength. Added strength gives not only muscles but also tendons and ligaments the ability to absorb impact and remain uninjured. It furthermore increases one's ability to rebound from the absorption of impact and in turn deliver forces against the ground that start movement, change direction, and improve reactivity.

HOW TO BUILD STRENGTH

Strength is achieved by overloading the muscles with and adapting them to unaccustomed stresses. As the following exercises illustrate, when training for strength it is better to utilize mass muscle groups than to isolate each separate muscle. This is because most sports do not require individual muscles to work separately, but rather that mass muscle groups work together. Tennis is such a sport.

PHYSICAL FITNESS FOR TENNIS KINETICS. . . . .

192

How to Perform Strength Exercises

It is imperative that you warm up and stretch before performing the strength exercises in this section. Never perform them while your muscles are cold. Follow these guidelines:

1. Perform just the number of sets and repetitions suggested for each exercise. Remember: More is not necessarily better (and could be worse).

2. If you add resistance (weights) while performing the exercises, do not add so much weight that technique becomes compromised.

3. Progress slowly. As with flexibility, strength is not achieved overnight.

4. Perform your strength exercises every *other* day. Not more than three times per week.

A precautionary word: Hours and sometimes even a day or two after exercising for strength, your muscles may feel sore. This is to be expected, since you may be exercising muscles that are unused to stress. If, however, pain and not soreness occurs during or after the exercise session, discontinue the pain-inducing exercise. *You must be able to distinguish between pain and soreness.* Soreness and discomfort will abate as you become more flexible and develop proper technique. Pain persists. If you experience pain, check your technique and make sure you are doing the exercises properly. If the pain still continues even with proper technique, check with your doctor.

**LOWER-BODY STRENGTH
EXERCISES**
. . . .

1. The quarter squat (muscle groups involved: quadriceps, hamstrings, hip abductors and adductors, and gluteal muscles).

Stand erect with hands on hips, feet planted shoulder width apart and turned outward approximately thirty degrees. Lower the body to a tennis Ready Position by bending *both* the hips and the knees (it is all right for the trunk to bend forward slightly), and return to the starting position.

2. The half squat (muscle groups involved: same as above). This exercise is performed in the same manner as the quarter squat, but the angle formed at the knee joint is now ninety degrees. It is important to bend as much from the hips as from the knees, and that the knees do not extend beyond the toes. The trunk may bend as much as sixty degrees forward.

3. The split (lunge) squat

(muscle groups involved: mainly the quadriceps and hamstring muscles, with some involvement of the hip abductors and adductors, and gluteal muscles). Standing erect, place the left leg forward with hip and knee slightly bent. Extend the right leg straight back. With trunk erect and hands on hips, lower the body until a ninety-degree angle is achieved at the left knee and hip. (The left knee should not extend beyond the toes of the left foot; if it does, place the foot farther forward and begin again). Repeat the exercise, switching leg positions.

4. The side (lunge) squat

(muscle groups involved: mainly the quadriceps, hamstrings, and hip abductors, with some involvement from the hip adductors and gluteal muscle groups). Stand erect with feet spread about one foot beyond shoulder width. Lean slowly to the right (keeping your upper body straight) until the right ankle, knee, and hip are in a straight vertical line. (The right knee should not extend beyond the toes of the right foot). Return to the starting position and repeat, this time leaning to the left.

5. The split squat walk. Stand erect, placing the left leg forward to form a ninety-degree angle at the knee and hip, keeping the right leg extended straight back. Place both hands on hips. Without raising the position of the upper body or leaning forward, walk by bending the hips and knees (to the same extreme angle) as the legs change position. With each stride the front and rear legs mimic the starting position. Begin by walking ten feet at a time, progressing gradually to thirty-foot walks.

6. The overhead snatch squat (muscle groups involved: quadriceps, hamstrings, hip abductors, hip adductors, gluteals, calves, and back extensors). A tennis racket is needed to perform this exercise. Feet are shoulder width apart and toes are pointed straight ahead. The back is arched and the trunk is bent slightly forward (approximately thirty degrees). The hips and knees are bent until both hands are at (or just above) the knees. Grasp the racket as shown.

With arms kept straight, "explode" upward with the legs and hips until the racket reaches waist level. At this point "shrug" the shoulders (without bending the arms) and continue to pull the racket straight up against the body until you are standing fully erect, both arms overhead.

This is an explosive exercise. Your heels may leave the floor at the start of the exercise, but the rest of your foot retains contact. The racket is raised with the forces from the legs and hips. The arms do not act until the racket is at lower-chest level.

**UPPER-BODY STRENGTH
EXERCISES**
....

7. Push-ups (muscle groups involved: pectoral muscles, anterior deltoid, triceps). Lie face down with the palms of your hands flat on the floor and slightly outside the shoulders. Keeping the body straight, push down on the hands, raising the body until the arms are straight. In this position the body weight should be on the hands and toes. Lower the body until it is one inch from the floor, and immediately repeat exercise.

Modification for the push-up: If the push-up is too difficult to perform as stated, keep your knees on the ground.

8. Shoulder (rotator cuff) exercises (muscle group involved: rotator cuff of the shoulder). Wrist weights or dumbbells will be needed to perform the following exercises:

External rotation. Lie on your left side with the weight in your right hand. The right elbow is in contact with your right side, bent at a ninety-degree angle. Turn the arm upward and try to extend the hand straight up. Return to the starting position. Repeat the exercise, lying on your right side with weight in the left hand.

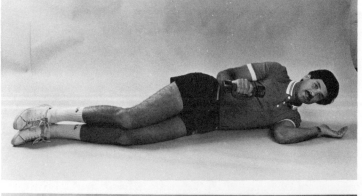

Internal rotation. Lie on your back with the weight in the right hand. The elbow is in contact with the right side of the body and is at a ninety-degree angle. Turn your arm inward in an attempt to touch the left side of your chest with the weight. Repeat the exercise with the weight in the left hand.

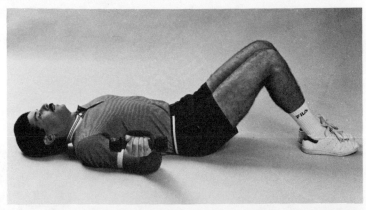

Rotator cuff exercise. Stand erect, and hold weights in each hand with thumbs pointed downward. Keeping arms straight and forward about thirty degrees from the body, raise both arms to shoulder level. Keep the thumbs pointed down, and do not raise the weights above the shoulders. Return to the starting position.

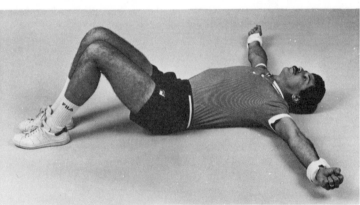

9. Chest flys (muscle groups involved: pectorals, anterior deltoid). Lie on your back with arms extended sideways, elbows straight. With weights in both hands and arms straight, raise hands until both meet directly over the chest.

10. Bent-over flys (muscle groups involved: posterior deltoid, rhomboids, latissimus dorsi). Stand with feet shoulder width apart. The trunk is bent forward sixty degrees, and there is a slight bend in both knees. Weights are held in each hand, both arms hanging straight down.

With elbows straight, bring up both arms until they are aligned with the shoulders. Return to the starting position.

11. Triceps press (muscle group involved: triceps). Weight is in the left hand. With forearm bent back, place the upper left arm against the left side of the head. Holding it in place with the right hand, extend the left forearm until it points straight up. Repeat this exercise with the weight in the right hand.

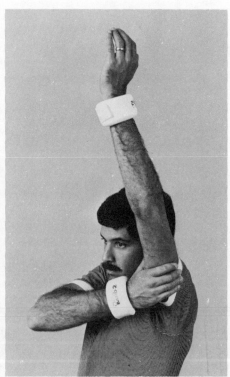

TRUNK EXERCISES

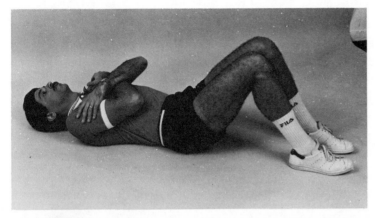

12. Sit-ups (muscle group involved: rectus abdominus). Lie on your back with knees bent at a ninety-degree angle. Cross the arms over the chest and place hands on opposite shoulders. Bring your chin to your chest and continue to curl forward until both shoulder blades are off the ground. Hold this position for three seconds, then return to the starting position.

Variation: Place hands behind your head.

13. Trunk twist (muscle groups involved: internal and external oblique). With lower body holding the tennis Ready Position, place a broomstick behind your neck and across both shoulders. With both hands over the broomstick, twist right, then left. (One twist to each side represents a repetition.)

PHYSICAL FITNESS FOR TENNIS KINETICS. . . . .

202

14. Abdominal leg thrusts (muscle groups involved: rectus abdominus, hip flexors, hip extensors). Lie on your back with arms at your sides and palms facing down. Keep the right leg straight while you bring the left knee to your chest. Switch leg positions by drawing the right leg to your chest while thrusting the left leg to a straight position. This is not a bicycling motion: The legs must move in a straight plane. Each time a knee touches the chest, one repetition is performed. To progress, perform this exercise with a twisting motion, bringing the left shoulder to the right knee and the right shoulder to the left knee.

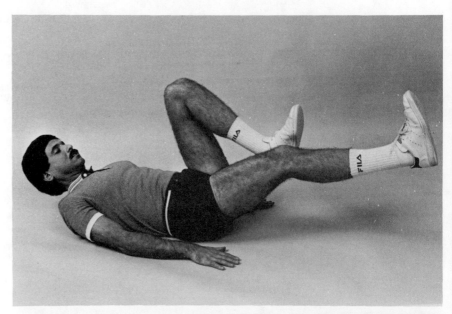

15. **Ninety-degree twists** (muscle groups involved: external and internal oblique muscles, rectus abdominus muscles). Sit on the floor with knees and trunk assuming a ninety-degree angle. Place both feet under an immovable object for extra support. Hold both arms extended directly in front of your chest with interlocked fingers, and twist to the right and to the left with the trunk (not the arms). One twist to the right and left counts as one repetition. Progression 1: Hold weights in both hands. Progression 2: Lean back so that the trunk assumes a forty-five-degree angle to the ground.

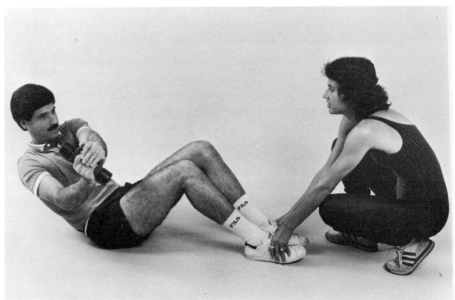

PHYSICAL FITNESS FOR TENNIS KINETICS. . . . .

204

Plyo (medicine) Ball toss (muscle group involved: rectus abdominus). *This is an advanced exercise and should be used last in the progression of abdominal exercises* (See cycle 3, p. 228).

Two people sit on the floor with interlocking ankles, as shown. One partner holds a medicine ball (see "plyometrics" in the pages that follow) overhead and performs a straight-armed sit-up. From the force generated by the abdominal muscles (not the arms) she releases the ball to her partner, who catches it and throws it back in the same manner.

The Plyo Ball is a modern medicine ball, soft and pliable on the outside with a liquid center, which provides resistance for dynamic, total body exercise. Plyo Balls are coded in high-visibility colors to indicate five-, seven- and nine-pound weights (manufactured by Triangle Bond Inc., Raleigh, N.C.).

. . . . STRENGTH

205

ADDING RESISTANCE TO THE STRENGTH EXERCISES

If you feel that you can get more out of these exercises by adding resistance, check yourself out with a few questions:

1. Am I currently performing the exercises properly?

If your technique is incorrect without resistance, it is important that you correct yourself before adding weight to the exercise. There is no substitute for technique. It not only exercises the muscles properly but also reduces the risk of injury. Before adding resistance, check your technique in a mirror or do the exercises with a discriminating partner.

2. Can I currently perform the suggested number of sets and repetitions?

If your answer is no, do not attempt to add resistance to the exercises. Again, concentrate on technique. The weight of your body and limbs is resistance enough to improve strength. Eventually you will be able to perform the suggested number of sets and repetitions, and only then consider adding resistance.

3. Am I currently operating without pain?

The presence of pain cannot go unheeded. If you feel pain without resistance, you will feel agony with it. Go no further.

If you answered yes to all three questions, you are ready to add resistance to the exercises. Begin with a two- to three-pound weight, performing ten repetitions (cuff weights for the legs, dumbbells or cuff weights for the hands). If you are not successful with this weight increment, decrease to a one-pound weight and repeat the process. If you are successful, experiment: Keep adding weights for the exercises until you find the one that enables you to complete the exercise with some difficulty *but without straining*. Don't go crazy with the weights. With good technique, higher resistance will follow. When the resistance you decide on becomes easy for you, add two-and-a-half pounds and repeat the process.

18 POWER

Strength and power are often mistaken as the same thing, but they are not synonymous. Strength deals with maximum muscle force. If somebody can lift ten pounds, then his strength would be recorded as such—ten pounds. Power is the work that is performed in a specific period of time. It is expressed as:

$$\frac{\text{Force} \times \text{Distance}}{\text{Time}} \quad \text{or} \quad \frac{\text{Work}}{\text{Time}}$$

Let's go back to the ten-pound weight. If a man raises the ten pounds five feet in two seconds, his power would be expressed as:

$$\frac{10 \times 5}{2} = \begin{array}{l} \text{25 foot-pounds of force developed} \\ \text{per second.} \end{array}$$

Decreasing the time element increases the output of power, so if the ten pounds is lifted five feet in one second instead of two, the foot pounds would equal fifty. The performance of a task in less time makes for a faster, quicker, and more forceful performance. That is why power training relies on velocity and explosiveness— on the excitation of muscles for a more powerful contraction. Tennis players need this power. If a player cannot move at great speed, or if he loses balance or control of his body at higher speeds, he will be a limited competitor. That is why Tennis Kinetics stresses explosive movement.

There is an effective training system that increases power production from the "ground up," just like the Tennis Kinetics chain of movement. It is called *plyometrics*. Plyometric exercises teach the tennis player to utilize the force of gravity to store energy within his muscular system. This stored energy is immediately used to produce explosive movement about the court.

Plyometric exercises can be tailored specifically for tennis. This sort of specificity of training, first developed in Eastern Europe, has become recognized as the most effective and efficient way to train for most any sport. Since its initial exposure to American track-and-field athletes, plyometric training has also made its way into the training regimens of professional football, basketball, and baseball players.

Cardiovascular conditioning is a valuable part of plyometric training, which helps to develop both aerobic and anaerobic abilities. Anaerobic training is basically concerned with the use of existing energy supplies within muscle tissue, and relies on recovery time to replenish these stores. Aerobic training brings the individual to a steady state of energy utilization and production through the intake of oxygen and metabolic function. The two seem mutually exclusive, but through proper training the anaerobic system can be taxed in a way that significantly increases the endurance and stamina of the athlete. This results in a higher threshold for anaerobic activity while allowing gains in the body's aerobic ability as well—perfect for tennis players, who are constantly asked to adapt to changes in direction (up and down, side to side, forward and back) at high speeds. The neuromuscular system must work together with the body's mass muscle groups in a balanced and coordinated fashion in order to create smooth and harmonious movement. Through plyometric training a player can train his body to work at high speeds with quickness, coordination, and balance.

PHYSICAL FITNESS FOR TENNIS KINETICS. . . . .

208

LOWER-EXTREMITY PLYOMETRICS

1. Hip kickers. The name says it. Lean forward slightly while keeping your back straight, and run in place with knees pointed straight down. Try to kick your heels into your buttocks. Each leg kick represents a repetition.

2. Quick foot drill. Assume the tennis Ready Position. Run quickly in place, keeping your feet close to the ground. Go all out, pumping with your arms—one or two runs at thirty-second intervals.

3. Split squat jumps. Assume the starting position of the split squat walk (strength exercise 5). Bounce in place twice, about six inches off the ground, then explode upwards. Land in the split squat position and repeat the jump. Each jump counts as one repetition.

PHYSICAL FITNESS FOR TENNIS KINETICS. . . . .

210

4. Split squat jump with cycling. Assume the SSJ position. Perform the SSJ, only this time switch the postions of the front and back legs. Upon landing, bounce twice and repeat the exercise.

5. Double-leg tuck jumps. Stand in the tennis Ready Position. Jump up, bending the hips and thighs until the thighs are parallel with the floor, briefly grasp both knees with your hands, then extend the legs to the floor. The instant the feet touch ground, repeat the jump. Each jump counts as one repetition.

6. Cone jumps. A six-inch cone is needed to perform this exercise.

Stand with the cone at your side. Jump side to side over the cone.

Stand behind the cone in the Ready Position. Jump forward over the cone and, as soon as you've landed, jump backward over it.

7. Double-leg hops. Stand in the Ready Position, hips and knees bent, and with your arms held back. Bounce a few times, then jump as far forward as possible. Use your arms! You should absorb the shock of the jump evenly, with both legs.

PHYSICAL FITNESS FOR TENNIS KINETICS. . . . .

214

8. Multiple double-leg hops. Perform as above, but the instant your feet hit the floor, perform another hop.

9. Standing triple jump. Stand in the ready position. Jump as you would for a double-leg hop (use your arms), and as you land on one foot, immediately hop to the other, then hop forward again, landing on both feet.

10. Cone hops. A number of cones are needed for this exercise, their height and number depending on one's level of skill. Place the cones in a straight line, two to three feet apart. Perform the cone jump exercise, going straight over each cone. Immediately upon landing, jump over the next one. Use your arms! Progression: Perform side jumps over the cones, tracing a diagonal path (side to side) as you progress over the cones.

PHYSICAL FITNESS FOR TENNIS KINETICS . . . .

216

11. Zigzag hops. Draw parallel lines on the ground, approximately twenty-four inches apart. Assume the Ready Position with your left foot on the right line. Explode off the floor, jumping diagonally to the left and landing on the opposite line with your left foot. Spring back immediately, jumping diagonally to the starting line. Repeat with the right foot, jumping to the left line. As you improve, move the lines farther apart—thirty, then thirty-six inches. Each jump counts as a repetition.

12. Lateral hop with step. This exercise requires a two-foot-by-two-foot box eight inches high (as one improves, the height of the box should increase to twelve inches). Assume the Ready Position, but with the right foot placed on top of the box. Explode vertically off the left foot landing with the right foot on the ground and the left on the box, and continue quickly and lightly. Each time one foot contacts the box, a repetition is performed.

13. In-depth jumps. This series of exercises is designed to utilize the tennis player's body weight and force of gravity to exert a force against the ground. These exercises develop the ability of a player to transfer stored energy into kinetic energy by landing, then jumping again as rapidly as possible. It uses the same box as in exercise 12: two feet by two feet by eight inches. Stand on top of the box. *Step* off the box (do not jump!) and as soon as both feet touch the ground, explode vertically.

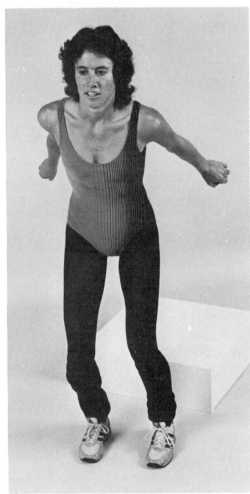

PHYSICAL FITNESS FOR TENNIS KINETICS. . . . .

218

VARIATIONS

Upon landing:

a. jump straight out as far as possible.

b. jump straight up, land, and run laterally to the left.

c. jump straight up, land, and run laterally to the right.

d. jump straight up, turn 180 degrees in the air before landing.

e. jump straight up, land, jump straight up again to a box of equal height.

Progression: Increase the height of the box in proportion to your improvement, up to 24″.

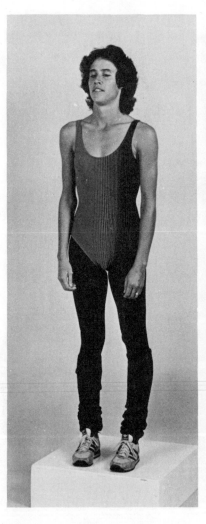
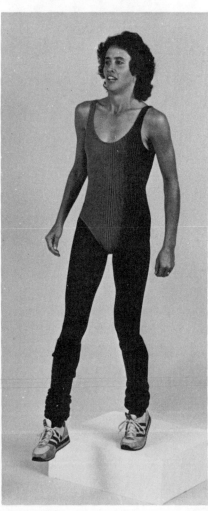
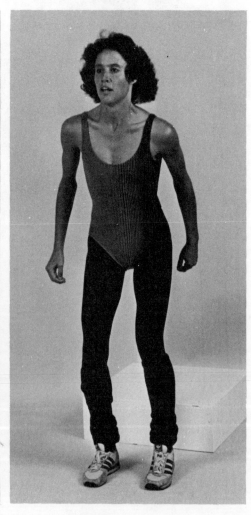

PHYSICAL FITNESS FOR TENNIS KINETICS. . . . .

220

f. In-depth jump with volley Cross-step. Perform the same in-depth jump as in the previous exercise, but upon landing perform the cross-step used in the volley.

PHYSICAL FITNESS FOR TENNIS KINETICS. . . . .

222

UPPER-BODY PLYOMETRICS

The following exercises are best done with the aid of a partner and a medicine ball or Plyo Ball. (As mentioned, the balls normally run in five-, seven-, and nine-pound increments; beginners and players who feel they lack upper-body strength should use the five-pound ball and advance slowly toward the heavier weights.)

If you have neither a partner nor a weighted ball, you can still perform the exercises, substituting a wall for the partner and a soccer or basketball for the weighted ball. As you master the techniques involved you can add wrist weights to supply the overload needed to develop strength and power. Continue to increase the wrist weights as you progress. *All of the following throws are done ten feet from your partner or wall.*

14. Chest pass. The emphasis should be placed on generating the forces of the legs and hips through the trunk and to the arms. Stand in the Ready Position. Hold the ball at the sides and lift it to chest level. Step forward with the left foot and throw the ball straight ahead. Complete the throw with arms fully extended and palms turned outward. Alternate the forward steps.

15. Overhead pass. Assume the same starting position as in the chest pass, but hold the ball directly over your head. Continue as in exercise 14.

16. Diagonal pass. Same starting position, but now the ball is held above and behind your right shoulder. Step forward with the left foot as you throw the ball diagonally over your right shoulder. It should pass above the shoulder so that a straight line could be drawn from the ball through the shoulder to the left hip.

As you complete the throw, bring the arms across and in front of the body while the trunk rotates to the left. At the end of the throw both arms should be extended with palms facing outward. Repeat the exercise by throwing over the left shoulder with the right foot forward.

17. Side pass. Follow the same procedure as that of the diagonal pass, with these exceptions:

a. Hold the ball top to bottom, not at the sides. If you are throwing from the right side, place the right hand on the bottom; vice versa from the other side.

b. Throw the ball from just above waist level. Again, remember to generate forces of the legs and hips through the trunk to the arms, and to employ good trunk rotation.

Note: All sets and repetitions are subject to change according to the cycle the individual is in, i.e., light Plyo Ball, eight to twelve repetitions in cycle 2; heavier Plyo Ball, twelve to fifteen repetitions in cycle 3, etc.

19 CYCLE TRAINING

You have now been introduced to all the exercises that constitute our program of fitness for Tennis Kinetics—exercises for strength and power (plus quickness, coordination, and balance), along with special stretching exercises for flexibility to combine with all your warm-ups. The time has come to organize these exercises into four cycles, per the charts in this chapter—cycles that will carry you through a year-round schedule of training. You exercise no more than two or three times a week, and no more than an hour in each full session (not counting warm-up and stretching), yet the benefits are at least the equal of daily generic programs of longer duration. The first three cycles are each performed for six to nine weeks; the fourth runs for twelve to sixteen weeks. The physiological systems of the body demand this much time to adapt to changes in stress.

Here are some guidelines to help you construct your own program:

1. The first cycle is designed to allow the body to adapt to stress, build tensile strength in tendons and muscles, and to cut down on body fat. Therefore this cycle should involve high numbers of repetitions of each exercise and should be done with submaximal intensity (lighter weights and resistance).

2. The second cycle consists of exercise routines, which call for higher resistance (increased weight) and fewer repetitions.

. . . . CYCLE TRAINING

227

Low levels of plyometric exercises should be introduced here.

3. The third cycle is when the body begins to develop the concept of power in movement. Many of the exercises in this chart are plyometric, done twice a week with higher repetitions. The overall strength exercises should be performed three times a week, using even fewer repetitions and near to maximum resistance.

4. The fourth cycle is a maintenance period. Exercise here is a blend of overall body strengthening movements, combined with plyometric exercises (for upper and lower body) for the development of specific skills.

5. In performing the plyometric exercises prescribed in the cycles, some individuals may progress faster than others. If you are slow to progress, do not worry. Certain exercises may not be as suited as others to your rate of progress. Try the exercises at your own rate and build as you go along.

6. Before starting the exercises for any session of any cycle, remember to warm up and perform all of the stretching exercises.

CYCLE 1: PREPARATION, SIX TO NINE WEEKS

(3 Exercises) Lower-Body Strength	(4 Exercises) Upper-Body Strength	(3 Exercises) Trunk
1. Quarter squat*	1. Push-ups	1. Sit-ups
2. Split lunge squat	2. Internal rotation	2. Trunk twist
3. Side lunge squat	3. External rotation	3. Abdominal leg thrusts
	4. Rotator cuff exercise	
3 sets of 10 repetitions. 3 times/week	2–3 sets of 10 repetitions. 3 times/week	2–3 sets of 12–15 repetitions. 3 times/week

*At week 3 in the cycle replace quarter squat with the half squat.

CYCLE 2: STRENGTH, SIX TO NINE WEEKS

UBS — Upper-Body Strength   UBP — Upper-Body Plyometrics
LBS — Lower-Body Strength   LBP — Lower-Body Plyometrics
ABD — Trunk Exercises

(4 Exercises) LBS	(4 Exercises) UBS	(4 Exercises) LBP	(2 Exercises) UBP	(4 Exercises) TRUNK (ABD)
1. Half squat 2. Split lunge squat 3. Split squat walk 4. Side lunge squat	1. Push-ups 2. Chest flys 3. Bent-over flys 4. Triceps press	1. Hip kickers 2. Double-leg hop *3. Split squat jumps 4. Split squat jumps with cycling; progress to multiple double-leg hops (3 sets of 3 repetitions, not 2 sets of 8–12).	1. Chest pass 2. Overhead pass	1. Sit-ups 2. Abdominal leg thrusts 3. Ninety-degree twists, progressing to forty-five degrees at week 4 or 5 4. Trunk twists
3 sets of 5–6 repetitions. Add wrist/ankle weights for increased resistance. three times/week (every other day)		2 sets of 8–12 repetitions. two times/week	2 sets of 8–12 repetitions. two times/week	2–3 sets of 12–15 repetitions. three times/week (every other day)

*At week 3 replace split squat jumps (page 209, #3) with split squat jumps with cycling (page 210, #4).

CYCLE 3: POWER, SIX TO NINE WEEKS

(5 Exercises) LBS	(4 Exercises) UBS	(5 Exercises) LBP	(4 Exercises) UBP	(5 Exercises) TRUNK
1. Half squat 2. Split lunge squat 3. Side lunge squat 4. Overhead snatch squat 5. Split squat walk	1. Push-ups 2. Bent-over flys 3. Rotator cuff 4. Triceps press	1. Double-leg tuck jumps 2. Jumps over cones 3. Zig-zag hops 4. Lateral hop with step 5. At week 3 add standing triple jumps (1 set of 8)	1. Overhead pass 2. Diagonal pass (right and left) 3. Side pass (right and left) 4. Chest pass	1. Sit-ups 2. Abdominal leg thrusts 3. Forty-five-degree twists 4. Abdominal toss with Plyo Ball 5. Trunk Twists
4 sets of 3–4 repetitions with added resistance. 3 times/week	4 sets of 3–4 repetitions with added resistance. 3 times/week	2 sets of 12–15 repetitions. 2 times/week	2 sets of 12–15 repetitions. 2 times/week	2–3 sets of 12–15 repetitions. 3 times/week

NOTE: When you reach this cycle, hip kickers and the quick foot drill should replace jogging in place for the warm-up.

CYCLE 4: MAINTENANCE, TWELVE TO SIXTEEN WEEKS

(4 Exercises) LBS	UBS	LBP	UBP	TRUNK
1. Quarter squat 2. Split lunge squat 3. Overhead squat 4. Side lunge squat	Choose 4 exercises from the list of seven upper-body strength exercises • Push-ups • External rotation • Internal rotation • Rotator cuff • Chest flys • Bent-over flys • Triceps press	In-depth jumps rotating in progressions, step a to f (see pages 217–221). Stay with 3 variations, changing them every 3 weeks.	3 of the 4 upper-body plyometric exercises • Chest pass • Overhead pass • Diagonal pass • Side passes	Choose 4 exercises from the trunk strengthening program • Sit-ups • Trunk twist • Abdominal leg thrusts • Ninety-degree twists • Plyo Ball toss
5–8 repetitions. 2–3 times/week	5–8 repetitions. 2–3 times/week	1 set of 10 repetitions for each variation. 1–2 times/week	1 set of 10 repetitions for each variation. 1–2 times/week	12–15 repetitions. 2–3 times/week

YEAR-ROUND TRAINING WITH ACTIVE REST

The final component of your year-round program of fitness for Tennis Kinetics is *active rest*. This means just what it says: take a break from the rigors of training, but remain active. Six to nine weeks for each of the first three cycles is ample time for them to serve their purposes, for both tennis development and physical fitness; more, and you are risking staleness and fatigue. The athlete should allow himself the luxury of letting his body recover and restore itself between cycles. And after twelve to fifteen weeks of the less demanding maintenance cycle, a longer sabbatical, here at the end of the entire program, provides needed rest before beginning the next schedule at higher intensity.

Activities during these periods should consist of a change of game (to golf, racquetball, jogging, swimming, etc.), house and garden projects, hiking or bicycling, or even a lighter schedule of tennis (without kinetic drills). Active rest prevents abuse of the body and allows for recovery. This can go a long way in maximizing training effects and preventing injuries.

Here, then, is how your training program comes together.

APPROXIMATE YEAR-ROUND TRAINING SCHEDULE
(AR = Active Rest)

Preparation 6–9 Wks.	Strength 6–9 Wks.	Power 6–9 Wks.	Maintenance 12–16 Wks.
	AR 1 Wk	AR 1 Wk	AR 1 Wk	AR 3–4 Wks

You then begin a new schedule, skipping over the preparation cycle and practicing the others at higher intensity—with increased weights/resistance.

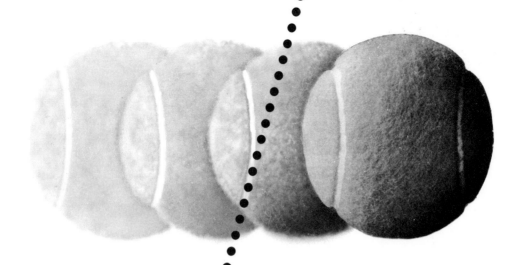

Four

MATCH PLAY

20 THE PREMATCH WARM-UP

For peak performance and injury prevention in match play, you must be well warmed up before you strike the first ball. We suggest that even before stepping on the court you spend a few minutes in front of a mirror, practicing the proper rhythms and kinetic chains until they feel natural and automatic. With no tennis balls to distract you and rush cold muscles, you will help get your body relaxed, poised, and ready to take the court.

Oddly enough, a good tennis player requires longer time to warm up than does a weak player. Think about it. From what you have learned about the body's chain of power you know that the large muscle systems take longer to fire than the smaller or quick systems that are taxed by lesser players. A good way to awaken *all* the moving parts is with shadow drills in front of a full-length mirror. Practice each kinetic stroke without running. Go through your groundstroke rhythms first, then move to your volleys, including the overhead. After that, practice groundstrokes in motion, return-of-serve rhythms, and the serving rhythm. Now you can take to the court.

The limited time for most prematch warm-ups requires you to be organized and thoughtful about your preparation. What should your court warm-up accomplish? Ideally these few minutes before the start of the match is the time for you to integrate those variables of your game over which you have control—Tennis Episodes, rhythms, and footwork—with the one key variable in tennis over which you have limited control—the oncoming ball. In the course of practice and development you can make the kinetics of your game as near to automatic as possible, but what can never be automatic is your ability to react to the ball, which is a different proposition every time. Just as a sprinter must be poised and ready for the starting gun to sound, a tennis player must be poised and ready for the ball at the moment it strikes the strings of the opponent's racket.

The prematch warm-up should get you moving quickly and efficiently to every ball. A brief review and breakdown:

1. **Be ready physically,** with knees bent, back straight, weight on the balls of your feet, head still. Watch the ball off your opponent's racket.

2. **Transition technique:** While you may not be able to produce perfect Tennis Episodes right away, if you turn your hips and shoulders, making your cross-steps and reacting right off the mark, you will be building up your kinetics and stroking skills. Just as it is imperative that you see the ball make contact on your opponent's strings, be sure you see its bounce on your side of the court. At that moment the ball is changing its height, speed, direction, and spin.

3. **Your strokes** should not be forced or hit very hard at first. Develop instead a feeling of lifting the ball and producing a smooth kinetic stroke. The four characteristics of a ball traveling through the air are *height, speed, spin,* and *direction*. Height is the most important characteristic by far because it produces depth. By controlling the height of a ball you are controlling your angles, lobs, long, looping groundstrokes, and low-flying passing shots. Most tennis players hit short into the court; one of the most basic fears in tennis is that of hitting the ball long. If you hit short in the warm-up you are only making it more difficult to add length in the match. Control the height of the ball right from the start.

4. **Take your volleys.** The key to the volley is the Reaction phase. As with the groundstrokes, you should go for depth on your volleys. If you are able to control the deep volleys, you will be able to make the soft, feathery angles as well. To practice short volleys during the prematch warm-up is unfair to your opponent, since he must then shag down the loose

balls during those few precious minutes before the match begins.

5. **On your overheads** (and you should ask for some lobs) the first step is the key step. Keep your racket up in a solid hitting position, and hit your smashes deep into the court. If time permits, aim a few into the short court, but again, establishing depth is paramount. When your opponent takes the net for some volleys, lower your sights and adjust the height of the ball for passing shots.

6. **The serve:** The key here is to keep the rhythm smooth and, again, to hit with depth into the service box. Warm up your second serve first and slowly build power. Remember that power on the serve comes from the kinetic chain. And do not feel as though you must show your opponent a monster serve in the warm-up. *Power comes from a chain.* You will probably need a few service games before you are hitting your hardest serves. In the warm-up, keep the racket head moving slowly so that it does not run away from your body until the last moment. If you let your arm whip early, it will be out in front of your body with little support and control, causing the racket face to jerk upon contact.

7. **Return-of-serve and approach shots:** If you are fortunate enough to have a coach or a friend willing to work with you before the match, be sure to address the return-of-serve and approach shot—two vital parts of the game that are often difficult to practice. If no such helper is available, or court time does not permit individual practice, ask your opponent for a few short balls so that you can follow the ball to the net. As for returns, we suggest, if your opponent is willing, that instead of launching into your own serves right away, you return his serves first. If you have the time, practice all possible returns—high up the middle, angles, short returns, and lob returns. If you are rushed for time, concentrate on a quick hip/shoulder turn and block the balls back up the middle of the court. The ball should be returned high against a baseliner and blocked low against a serve-and-volleyer, but in either case aim up the middle of the court. A return of serve to the court's center is as safe a return as you can hit, and very effective.

8. **If you find yourself** experiencing a case of nerves on the day of your match, remember to keep moving for the ball during the warm-up (and during the match itself). The most common occurrence on nervous days is to get slow-witted and lead-footed, so if you can concentrate on quick footwork and clean preparation, you can play yourself right out of such a nervous patch.

COMMON ERRORS OF THE WARM-UP

1. Focusing on the results and not the production of your strokes and movement. All too often a player will start to panic if he does not immediately find his range. This is very common, and very unnecessary. Instead of concerning yourself with lack of control, work on the things that will affect control of the ball. Focus on the cause, not the result of your efforts.

2. Trying to achieve too much power. One of the easiest ways to throw off your timing and control is to "think speed" in the warm-up. More often than not, this will produce a nonkinetic stroke, and you will find yourself having to struggle to find form through the entire match. Depth is the key in the warm-up. Do not go for power, and do not put an inordinate amount of importance on finding the corners of the court. With depth comes control.

3. Trying to study your opponent. Concern yourself first and foremost with your own game. Once you feel warmed up, you can take the time to analyze your opponent's style, but it should never be at the expense of your own game. Do not try to test him for weaknesses throughout the warm-up. Knowing his soft spots and devising strategies against them without the ability to utilize such knowledge leads to frustration and unnecessary losses. As the match proceeds, your opponent's game will become familiar to you, warts and all. At the same time, do not use your warm-up to work on your own faultiest shot. If you know you've got a suspicious-looking backhand, do not draw attention to it by asking your opponent for some extra shots to that wing. And if your opponent has a nifty drop shot that you lack, do not try trading that stroke with him. Stick to your game and use your strongest weapons to their fullest.

. . . . **THE PREMATCH WARM-UP**

237

4. Intimidating your opponent with your monster serve. Do not try to unleash the biggies right away. The going should be slow in the warm-up, with gradual increases of power as you go along. Keep your warm-up kinetic.

5. Trying to conserve energy. A casual warm-up will not warm you nearly enough for the match, and energy saving will only make the going a lot tougher when play begins. The warm-up sets the tone for the entire match, so make sure you prepare with full movement.

COURT SURFACE CONDITIONS

Regardless of the court surface, you should warm up in the style you will be using for your match. Certainly different surfaces place importance on different parts of your game. Clay courts bring out everyone's groundstrokes, while the faster, harder surfaces maximize the importance of serving, returns of serve, and volleys. On slow courts you should hit higher over the net. Balls get heavy on clay, collecting particles and moisture with each stroke, and rallies tend to go a lot longer on such surfaces. The ball will also get fuzzy, thereby increasing its resistance through the air. This means that you must hit the ball higher to have it go deeper. On a hard surface, just the opposite happens to the ball. It gets compressed, travels through the air faster, so you need to add spin and touch to your shots.

ENVIRONMENTAL CONDITIONS

Playing in the heat. If you try to conserve energy during your warm-up on a hot, sunny day, you could very well find yourself out in the heat a lot longer than you wish to be. Full running and stroke-by-stroke preparation are as important on a hot day as on any other, and perhaps more to the point, they can help get you off the court a bit sooner.

In the cold. Try to get a longer warm-up off the court on cold days, and to space out the warm-up with extra running and stretching. It takes the body more time to increase its core temperature and reach peak performance in the cold, so go slowly and avoid hard hitting. You may find on cold days that you lack touch in your hand and fingertips, so warm them well beforehand.

In the wind. Because of the extra likelihood of mishit balls on windy days, it is more important to produce kinetic strokes under such conditions than at any other time. You should keep the emphasis on quick footwork and early hip-and-shoulder turns. When you move to hit the ball, take extra care to watch the ball bounce, and get good body rotation to allow for the ever-shifting ball.

TEST THE STRENGTH OF YOUR TENNIS EPISODES

As we have mentioned throughout this book, you are only as good as your weakest link, so during the warm-up you should examine every element of each rhythm. Determine whether or not your movements are correct. Are there certain elements you perform better than others? Are you connecting one rhythm to another on time? Are your rhythms better from side to side than they are forward and backward? Remember that if you do not put your Tennis Episodes to the test, your opponent will. Smart players make a specialty of finding weaknesses and forcing their display during a match. So beat your opponent to the punch by finding the areas of weakness yourself. Correct any such troublesome elements of your game during the warm-up, so that you can play the match in the correct way, and automatically.

21 STRATEGY AND TACTICS

The time has come for your Tennis Kinetics payoff. You have learned about movement, rhythm, power, control. With the help of a few minutes' practice each day you have programmed your muscles and mind so that the game seems simple and entirely more fun to play. We have given you new concepts and new ways of playing the sport, and now it is time to put them to the test.

Through Tennis Kinetics, we have strived to make many complicated moves automatic and therefore simple, because we know that in a match filled with pressure the odds are that a player will not do what is not automatic. A player trying for an all-important passing shot will perform the play a lot better when he is not burdened with worry over the mechanics of the stroke. With Tennis Kinetics you will have committed many of the necessary moves to muscle memory, so that in a match you need concentrate only on the ball.

This chapter will illustrate how Tennis Kinetics theories are used in match situations. By producing quality Episodes and connecting your rhythms, you will be a much tougher competitor. Your opponent will notice, too.

MATCH PLAY . . . .

240

BASIC PLAY
. . . .

We have mentioned previously that in club-level tennis the odds are greater than eight to one that a rally will end in error; in the professional game, the odds are often greater than four to one. It is therefore important to develop a high-quality defensive game before going for winners. Every game needs a combination of both, and often a brilliant offensive rally is created with defensive savvy. (Watch the pros hoist a lob to bring forth a defensive return, then hammer the reply home for a winner, and you will recognize the necessary marriage of offense and defense.)

The two keys to connecting good, strong plays are well-timed split steps and short backswings. Navratilova and McEnroe make the best transfers from backcourt to forecourt, from defense to offense, and it is their powerful kinetic chains that allow them to use shorter backswings for more power and control. The classic defensive reply to a serve or volley is to chip low over the net. This asks the opponent to volley up on the ball; your defensive shot will have forced a weak reply. (Remember that for every winner hit there are eight errors!)

Another good defensive tactic is hitting crosscourt in rallies, especially when you are forced out of court. Down-the-line winners are breathtaking to watch and a lot of fun to make, but they are much more difficult to execute on the run, and they make the chance for recovery near impossible. Use down-the-line shots sparingly and cunningly, and remember that the percentages are with the alternative, which gives you more court area over a lower part of the net.

Use your lob. A lob can get you out of all sorts of trouble, and especially in club play the prospect of hitting overheads can strike terror in your opponent. We suggest that your lobs be hit with underspin, not topspin or flat. The lob is easier to lift with underspin, gives you a lot of feel for the ball, and can be produced in the most compromising situations—out of court, off balance, even behind your body.

If your opponent has a strong smash, you will want to take care that your lobs find his backhand side. The backhand smash poses problems for the finest players. The difference of a few inches in the direction of your lob will give your opponent either one of his favorite shots (forehand) or one of the hardest in the book (backhand).

A player's second serve is frequently the worst part of his game, and affects him much more than he may realize. A player with a weak second serve cannot be regarded as a complete player and despite an otherwise capable game, his glaring weakness can cost him good doubles partners.

In a match situation, the player with a weak second serve may find himself taking a lot off his first ball so that he will not have to resort to the second. This sort of accommodation nullifies the server's position of strength and takes the heat off the returner for both that game and the next (where he has the advantage of starting the point). Put plenty of spin on your second serve, and keep the ball deep enough so that you can stay out of the way of booming returns.

The best defense on returns of serve, at least initially, is straight up the middle of the court. As confidence grows, you'll want to move the ball around the court, and you may try to play some back with topspin if time permits and you can catch the ball out in front of your body. If the server hits a hard ball, your best play is to block the ball back deep. You do not want to "push" the ball—normally a pusher's shots lack length and conviction—but if you can keep the ball coming back to the hard hitter with depth, he may become discouraged and take speed off his deliveries.

The trick to taking the offense is that you want both power and the percentages to be with you. Hitting hard and going for winners do not by themselves constitute offensive plays; in fact they can be rather stupid tactics. If you find yourself in a *position* of strength, your percentages should remain high as you go after the point.

Your biggest potential offensive weapon is your serve. What you should note about two of the best servers in today's game, John McEnroe and Martina Navratilova, is that they place the premium on depth and angle, not power. When you aim well and strike the ball deep you give yourself an extra step into the net because the balls stay in the air that much longer. It is also much more difficult for an opponent to play back a serve that bounces close to him and pins him to the baseline. Slicing balls wide and short can pose problems for returners and give the server a lot of open court with which to play his next shot. Good placement of the serve to an opponent's weaker wing is also disconcerting and difficult to field.

A serve-and-volley player is better off hitting his first serve out than hitting it short. Why? Because if your first serve misses you have another serve coming that could put you in better stead. A short first serve spells trouble for the serve-and-volley player, who can more easily get passed trying to come in behind a serve that

MATCH PLAY . . . .

242

combines his own power with that of his opponent moving in on the shot.

The most basic offensive play on return of serve is to follow in on the weak deliveries. Take those balls as approach shots and slice deep and low. If the serve is strong, you may want to match power with power, but with the possible exception of Jimmy Conners there is no player who trades lightning bolts and keeps his percentages high. Your return of serve should be guided by the height of the ball and the position of your opponent. If he follows his service to the net, hit low to his feet, or if you are confident of your control, aim for the sides of the court. If he's a baseliner, keep him from making a strong response by giving yourself plenty of room to clear the net, trading depth for power.

OFFENSIVE GROUNDSTROKES

Once in a rare while you see cold, outright winners from the baseline, but their infrequency underscores the difficulty of the task. More important than blasting from the baseline is maneuvering the ball to all parts of the court and taking your shots on the rise. This tactic cuts down your opponent's time to think and execute. Yet very few players can play the early ball all the time without significantly reducing their percentages. We suggest that if you want to play your shots early, pick your spots with care. If you are at all rushed or somehow on the defensive, do not try to scare up an attacking on-the-rise surprise. From what you have learned in chapter 2 you will appreciate knowing that the closer the ball is to its bounce off the court, the more force it will impose on your racket. You must be well prepared to absorb the shock of such a heavy ball with quick preparation and a sound kinetic chain.

In the previous section we cautioned you on using down-the-line shots in defensive situations, but the same play can be a wonderful offensive move. Make certain to achieve a good amount of depth, or you will be staring down a crosscourt angle from a poisonous position on the court.

To break up a point with an element of surprise, or to tire an opponent, nothing can match a well-executed drop shot. The drop shot is strictly offensive in nature. For a drop shot to be effective the hitter must be faced with the choice of a drop, a groundstroke, or an approach shot, and he must be able to disguise his feathery touch to initially resemble his other options.

. . . . STRATEGY AND TACTICS

243

HOW TO CONTROL THE TEMPO

Great players have the ability to change and control the tempo of a match. Other than Jimmy Connors, who does this by consistently hard hitting, these top winners manage it by controlling the characteristics of a struck ball—its height, speed, spin, and direction. (Though Connors does a wonderful job of relentless slugging, a flat ball very often gives the opponent a chance to feed off one's power and rhythm.) With all the variables presented in any given court situation, the good player has a range of opportunities with which to provoke errors. You, too, with Tennis Kinetics, can take charge of the tempo of a match.

A vital part of controlling the characteristics of your shots is the way you move on court. Against a hard hitter you must get to the ball very early so that you have enough control to vary the pace of the ball on the next shot. Hard hitters usually enjoy playing other hard hitters, so instead, when facing such a player, mix in a lot of loops, dinks, and change-ups to throw off his timing and rhythm. Against a soft hitter you run the risk of getting lulled into the same slow cadence of your opponent's play, or of getting frustrated and switching to an anxious and helter-skelter game of hardball; either way you are apt to come up short. You can take the tempo away from a pusher by keeping your own game very tidy and by outrunning, outreacting, and outsteadying your opponent. If you find yourself losing the long rallies, go for plenty of depth and be ready to counter any short ball with an aggressive move toward the net. By moving your opponent out of his comfort zone and varying your movement, you can take control and keep it.

LEARN HOW TO TAKE ADVANTAGE OF SITUATIONS

Every point grants one of the players a prime opportunity to seize control, and the quality of that person's play will dictate whether or not he can exploit the chance. Many times the fortunate player who has been handed such a moment is unable to seize it—either because he has not recognized his chance or because he cannot produce the necessary finishing skills. Points can drag on and on for baseline players who cannot connect the groundstroke rhythm with the approach shot rhythm, or for return-of-servers who play every service, weak or strong, the same way. It is a terrible waste of time and effort to be capable of setting up the winning shot but then find yourself unable to finish the job. If you mean to be a total player, you must learn to end the point on your own terms.

How do you know when the time to strike is right? If your opponent is on the run, moving sideways, or stretching for a ball, make your move. Lean forward into the court and anticipate a weak reply. If your opponent is off the court, position according to the maps in chapter 3, and look to hit your next ball on the rise. If you are at the net, close in and take your volleys as early as possible. You want to cut off the angles quickly and efficiently, so aim for the open court or drop one just over the net. When answering a lob, your first step back is key. And you should be looking skyward whenever you pull your opponent very wide or very deep. Repositioning after your smash is also all-important—you may not finish the point on the overhead, but your next shot should.

FACING DIFFERENT LEVELS OF PLAY

What to Do against a Stronger Player than Yourself

Going into a match against a better player, two things must happen for you to win: You must play a very fine match, and your opponent must be off his own game. Frequently a weaker player who has put together a good match will come off the court and say, "I just went out there hoping not to make a fool of myself." He did not try to do more than he was capable of doing, as is so often the tendency, and ended up making it a close match, or even winning. The idea is to try to keep your opponent out there. Make him hit a lot of shots. The longer you keep a stronger opponent out on the court, the better your chance of victory. That holds true even against a steady baseline player. While he will want to play the long rallies against you, you should not try to win the points too early. If you do, you will usually find yourself attempting more difficult shots from weaker positions, never giving your opponent the chance to make an error of his own; in the end, you will just lose faster. Instead, try to make every return a high-quality Episode, and keep in mind that your best chance of winning is dependent upon your opponent's rate of errors. So do not rush your play, and try not to even think about your opponent's game. If you can keep your own level of play high and *steady*, you will find yourself playing your best tennis against a better player.

What to Do against a Weaker Player

Every match has a built-in measure of pressure, and the tendency of many players as they enter into a match against a weaker opponent is to underestimate the task of winning. They will squander points and leads or experiment with tactics and technique, often at their own expense. So the strategy of sticking to your own game in a match is even more important against a weaker player. Establish your rhythms right from the start and concentrate hard at the beginning of games and sets, when weaker players are more apt to catch stronger players off guard.

What to Do against an Opponent of the Same Level as Yourself

This is the most interesting proposition. Either player can win, and the slightest difference in concentration, confidence, or control can decide the winner. Interestingly enough, the scores of very even opponents will often seem decisive—6–2, 6–2, or 6–3, 6–1— but with the score itself hardly reflecting the struggle for victory. Against an equal you must show strength of character and a genuine willingness to stay on the court until you win. You must indicate continually that you are out there to work, for the player who remains mentally agile and is dogged about every point will wear his opponent down.

What this means is that you must create a certain image on the court: of a player who has in his power the ability to win every point from his equal. If a rally ends with the winning shot buzzing by you with ease, you have given off a very vulnerable impression. Indeed, the distance between you and the ball at point's end is a great indicator of your current strength in a match. If you end up ten feet from a winning shot, your opponent can feel pretty happy with himself. If, instead, your losing effort is only inches from the winning ball, you have applied the pressure to your opponent even in the loss of a point. So at all times, apply pressure with the most solid tennis you know how to play, and always keep trying!

RAISING YOUR LEVEL OF PLAY: A REMINDER

When most players decide that they must raise the level of their play during a match, they try to raise their level of hitting. This is a huge mistake. The moment of contact represents only one brief element of the Tennis Episode, and is the result of the other components of the Tennis Episode that precede it. To ask yourself to improve upon your hitting without improving the quality of everything else is foolhardy. We say this because if your goal is to hit the ball better, you may find that you do, in fact, strike a nice, clean ball, but the ball comes back anyway. Now what? The chances that you can continue to hit better and better are pretty slim because to hit harder, or sweeter, or earlier, or closer to the lines means that *you must get to the ball earlier*—that is, faster, with more balance and control. If you really want to raise your level of play, do not be nearsighted about your target. Focus on improving the quality of your entire Tennis Episode.

PERFORMING UNDER PRESSURE

The symptoms of a player under pressure are very visible: He looks stiff and awkward, his heels are on the ground, he's guessing madly instead of preparing and reacting, and he is obviously thinking of the opponent, not the ball. A person just learning to drive a car is in much the same state, thinking of the brakes, the gas pedal, his speed, hand signals, pedestrians, and traffic. Everything seems new and frightening, and nothing seems possible without conscious thought. A skilled driver, by comparison, has the capability of processing a lot of information very quickly, and under the pressure of icy roads or sheets of rain he makes the proper decisions and acts upon them, instantly.

A skilled tennis player reacts to crisis situations in the same manner. He has programmed his mind and body so well that the more complicated and pressure-filled the situation, the simpler it is for him to rise to the occasion and play the moment for all it's worth. When you know that you can call on your shots without thinking about them, the pressure is lifted from you and is placed squarely on the shoulders of your opponent. It is comforting to know that the longer a rally lasts, the stronger you get, and that the bigger the pressure, the lighter your load.

22 THE LOOK

We call this last chapter of the book "The Look" because it represents the ultimate look of Tennis Kinetics at the peak of match play. All of its photographs were shot at the Wimbledon final of 1984, an event in which I needed to be at the height of my powers to turn back Chris Evert Lloyd. As you will see time and again, I continually needed quick reactions and maneuverability to perform the necessary shots, and the principles of Tennis Kinetics had to be applied throughout the match. And they worked. I won.

Though you and I may not play with the same style, and though you may not get to perform on Centre Court at Wimbledon, we can share the joys and exultation of victory. That part of us is truly the same.

—Martina Navratilova

Reaction—Starting from a solid Ready Position, I intensify my concentration as my opponent prepares to serve. I try to stay balanced, poised, and ready to cover my opponent's serve.

Transition (forehand ground-stroke)—I really got behind this one. Obviously I am in a good hitting position: My weight is coming forward, and my foot-work is correct. I find that once my legs are in the proper position my upper body follows.

Transition (return of serve)—This serve must have been well struck, not leaving me time to get my feet in the proper position. Fortunately I can still turn my hips and shoulders.

Transition (backhand volley)—You can see by my position on the court that I am being forced to hit a tough first volley. I'm a bit off balance and cannot lean forward, so I make certain to get the most from a good shoulder turn. It isn't easy to stretch for a high volley such as this. You've just got to try to execute the shot as well as possible, then close in a lot tighter to the net for the second volley.

MATCH PLAY . . . .

250

Movement (a wide backhand)—
This is a good, basic, balanced backhand from the baseline, and I'm well set for a good shot. I'm in pretty good position, and my racket is back.

Serve—I'm getting low in the legs so that I can jump into the serve. There is so much power to be gotten from the legs, and so many players seem to underestimate that fact. And don't forget—a good serve starts with a good toss. The kinetic chain begins in the legs, goes to the hips, trunk, shoulders, arm, wrist, and racket.

Contact (close volley)—From this position I'm in the driver's seat. I love to hit a drop volley, especially on a surface like grass. The ball just dies.

Approach shot—You work for a shot like this. It's a standing approach shot, so there's a lot of control. I like replying to a high midcourt ball, and on this one my weight is forward and I'm contacting the ball pretty much in front, where I want to be hitting. I try to take advantage of short balls by attacking them early before they drop. (Many players let the ball fall below the height of the net and lose a good advantage.)

Contact (backhand ground-stroke)—Trouble. I'm late here, fading back and contacting out of a position of weakness—the ball is behind me. It's easy for this to happen on grass. I do have a few things going for me, though. I'm bending my knees and watching the ball.

Contact (low volley)—I'd always rather hit a low volley than a half volley, even though these shots are tough. The most important thing to remember is to hit them deep and force your opponent to play another ball. Try to go down the line—a crosscourt shot doesn't allow much time for Recovery.

Contact (backhand volley)—This is my sharp-angled crosscourt backhand volley—a favorite of mine. The same shot on my forehand side is not as good, but this is a high-percentage shot for me. I take the ball in front and keep my racket face firm at a fixed angle. I put a little bit of underspin on the ball to cut the shot and control it.